Illustrator:
Howard Chaney

Editor:
Janet Cain, M.Ed.

Editorial Project Manager:
Ina Massler Levin, M.A.

Editor in Chief:
Sharon Coan, M.S. Ed.

Art Director:
Elayne Roberts

Associate Designer:
Denise Bauer

Cover Artist:
Keith Vasconcelles

Product Manager:
Phil Garcia

Imaging:
Richard Yslava
Ralph Olmedo, Jr.

Publishers:
Rachelle Cracchiolo, M.S. Ed.
Mary Dupuy Smith, M.S. Ed.

P9-CKK-010

Math EXPLORATIONS

- **Pictographs**
- **Bar Graphs**
- **Line Graphs**
- **Coordinate Graphs**
- **Real Graphs**

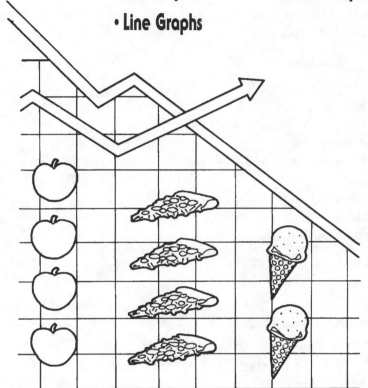

Authors:

Tina Tucker
Janet Cain, M.Ed.

Teacher Created Materials, Inc.
P.O. Box 1040
Huntington Beach, CA   92647
ISBN-1-55734-007-X

©1997 Teacher Created Materials, Inc.   Made in U.S.A.

Table of Contents

Table of Contents *(cont.)*

Introduction

Math Explorations is a 144-page resource book created specifically for primary students. Five types of graphs (pictographs, bar graphs, line graphs, coordinate graphs, real graphs) are presented. Students learn how to collect and organize different types of data, create graphs, and use graphs to interpret data. This book provides fun and exciting opportunities for students to apply graphing skills across the curriculum. Connecting curriculum areas is a popular trend in education with the goal of building a better understanding of math concepts while enhancing students' interest and making learning more meaningful. Students improve their basic math skills and are encouraged to be problem solvers by using techniques such as brainstorming, critical thinking, and cooperative learning. As they are introduced to new challenges, students will approach these tasks eagerly and enthusiastically.

Feel free to present these graphing activities in the way that best fits the needs of your students and your teaching style.

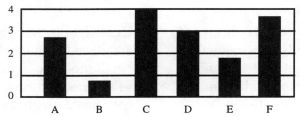

Types of Graphs

A graph is a picture that is used to organize information, called data, making it easier to understand. Five types of graphs are presented in this book: pictographs, bar graphs, line graphs, coordinate graphs, and real graphs. A description and illustration of each type of graph appears on this page.

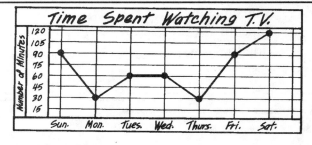

Pictograph: Pictures or symbols are used to present data. The title and type of pictures or symbols often tell what the graph is about. A key can be used to show the value of each picture or symbol.

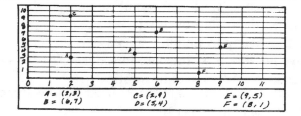

Bar Graph: Either horizontal or vertical bars are used to present data. The title describes what type of data is given in the graph. The labels along the bottom and side show how the data is organized. A bar graph makes it easier to compare data.

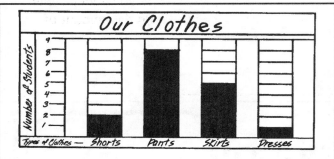

Line Graph: A line is used to show changes over time. When the line goes up, it is called an *increase*. When it goes down, it is called a *decrease*. The title tells what type of information is being presented. The labels along the bottom and side show the type of measurement and the period of time.

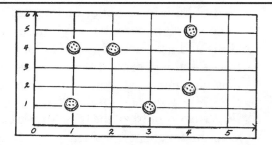

Coordinate Graph: Coordinates, or a pair of numbers, are used to tell the location of a point. Coordinates are written like this: (3, 4). The first number always tells how many units you should move to the right. The second number always tells how many units you should move up. The bottom left-hand corner of the graph is always (0, 0).

Real Graph: Manipulatives, or real objects, are placed on a graph. A real graph can be similar to a pictograph, with real objects substituted for the pictures, or it can be like a coordinate graph with real objects placed according to the number pairs.

Ways to Present Graphs

This book presents a variety of topics so that students can make and use graphs while studying different thematic units. Graphs that are large and easy to see can be created for the floor, wall, or bulletin board. These types of graphs are excellent tools for modeling new skills and motivating students to become active participants. To complete the graphing activities in this book, students can work as a class, in small groups, with partners, or independently.

Floor Graph: Use butcher paper, a large sheet of plastic or vinyl, or a flat bed sheet to create a floor graph. Draw the horizontal and vertical lines on the graph. If you are using butcher paper, laminate it. Cut out the pictures, symbols, or bars from colored construction paper that is laminated, plastic or vinyl, or fabric. Attach these to the floor graph with Velcro®, double-stick tape, or safety pins. Create line graphs, using colored yarn or string. Prevent the graph from slipping by attaching pieces of rubber to the back or by using duct tape to stick it onto the floor.

Wall Graph: This type of graph can be placed along a wall or on a bulletin board and used throughout the year. Create a wall graph, using the same materials as the floor graph. Velcro®, double-stick tape, staples, or tacks can be used to attach the pictures, symbols, bars, and lines. Be sure the graph is at a height students can reach. The size depends on the amount of space available.

Individual Graphs: Reproduce the graph forms in this book and have students use them for guided and independent practice. Encourage students to take their graphs home to share with their families.

Real Graph: This type of graph is easily created using paper or poster board. Help students create the graph. Then ask questions about it. You may wish to have students transfer the information from the real graphs to individual graphs.

Computer Resources: Several software manufacturers offer programs that can be used to help students learn about graphs. Following are a couple of suggestions.

- *The Graph Club* by Peggy Healy Stearns and Tom Snyder Productions. Software for MAC or Windows. Available from Tom Snyder Productions, 1-800-342-0236.

- *Graphers* by Lois Edwards Educational Design and Sunburst Communications. Software for MAC or Windows. Available from Sunburst Communications, P.O. Box 100, Pleasantville, NY 10570-0100, 1-800-321-7511.

Table

Title:	

Vertical Graph

Horizontal Graph

Coordinate Graph

Shapes

Preparation:

1. Reproduce the table (page 6) for students and make an overhead transparency of it.
2. Reproduce the large and small shape patterns (page 11) and the pictograph (page 12). Cut apart the shape patterns. Make one set of small shapes for each pair or group of students. The number of each type of shape can vary. Place the small shapes in reclosable plastic bags or envelopes, making all of the sets exactly the same.

Directions:

1. Use the large patterns to review the names and distinguishing features of the different shapes.
2. Have students help you count the number of each large shape. Use the overhead transparency to record the data, as shown in the following example.

SHAPES	
Shapes	**Number of Shapes**
Circle	3
Triangle	4
Square	5
Rectangle	2
Pentagon	3
Hexagon	1

3. Use the floor or wall graph to model the activity. Make the key: 1 Picture = 1 Shape. Have students place the large shapes in the appropriate sections of the graph, making sure they are aligned vertically.
4. Divide the class into small groups or assign partners. Have students count the small shapes in the bags and record the data on their tables. Then have them glue the shapes on their pictographs. Remind them to align the shapes so that the graph is easy to read.
5. Discuss the questions (page 12) and ask additional ones to check students' understanding.

Extension Activities:

1. Have students brainstorm a list of objects in the classroom that are the same shapes as the ones used in this activity.
2. Teach students about probability, using the shapes. After determining the number of each shape, have students replace them in the bags or envelopes. Then have students make predictions about which shapes are most likely, least likely, or equally likely to be drawn. *(The shape with the greatest number will most likely be drawn. The one with the fewest will least likely be drawn. Shapes that have the same number will have an equal chance of being drawn.)*
3. Reproduce the small shape patterns (page 11) for students. Let them create pictures by gluing the shapes onto construction paper and coloring them.
4. Have students create real graphs, using three-dimensional shapes such as spheres, cubes, cylinders, and cones.

Shapes (cont.)

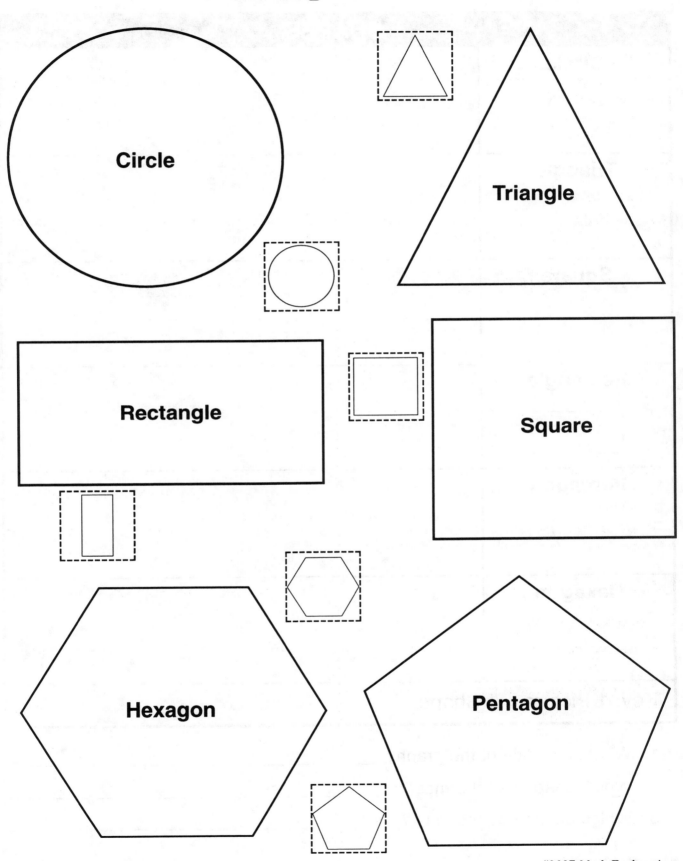

Circle

Triangle

Rectangle

Square

Hexagon

Pentagon

#2007 Math Explorations

Shapes *(cont.)*

SHAPES	
Circle	
Triangle	
Square	
Rectangle	
Pentagon	
Hexagon	
Key: 1 Picture = 1 Shape	

1. What is the title of the graph? _____

2. Which shape has the most? _____

3. Which shape has the least? _____

12

Apples

Preparation:

1. On a day that you specify, have students bring two differently colored apples.
2. Reproduce the large and small apple patterns (page 14). Give each student about 20 small apple patterns and three large apple patterns (red, green, yellow). Reproduce and make an overhead transparency of the pictograph (page 15).
3. Obtain a large basket such as the type used for laundry.

Directions:

1. Place the apples that students bring to class in the large basket. Be sure that the apples are not grouped by color.
2. Allow students to take turns looking in the basket. Concurrently, have them cut apart the apple patterns. Ask students to color their large apples according to the labels, using red, green, and yellow crayons or markers. Tell them not to color the small apples yet.
3. Invite students to make predictions about the apples in the basket, using the following statement: *We have mostly _____ apples.* Have each student select the large apple pattern that matches his/her color prediction.
4. Ask students to place their large apple patterns on the wall or floor graph according to their predictions. Remind them to align the apples so that the graph is easy to read. On a floor graph, you may wish to use a real apple to mark each row.
5. To make the key, trace a large apple pattern. Show that one apple pattern represents one vote. Discuss the results of the graph.
6. Explain to students that predictions can be changed as new information is revealed. Now choose volunteers to help you sort the apples according to colors. Without counting the apples, give students the opportunity to change their predictions on the graph. Ask volunteers to explain why they changed their predictions.
7. Together count how many apples are in each group. Use an overhead transparency to record the data.
8. Show students how to count by twos to compress the data. Tell them that half of an apple pattern would represent one real apple. Use the transparency of the pictograph to demonstrate. On the key, show that each apple pattern represents two real apples.
9. Have students glue the small apple patterns on their pictographs (page 15) according to the data on the transparency. Remind them that the apples should be aligned so that the graph is easy to read. Depending on the row the patterns are in, ask them to color the apples red, green, or yellow. As an alternative, students can use apple stickers (TCM 1246) to create the pictograph.

Extension Activities:

1. Have students brainstorm a list of objects that are red, green, and yellow in the classroom.
2. Allow students to taste each type of apple. Invite them to vote on their favorite types of apples. Have them show the data on pictographs.

Apples *(cont.)*

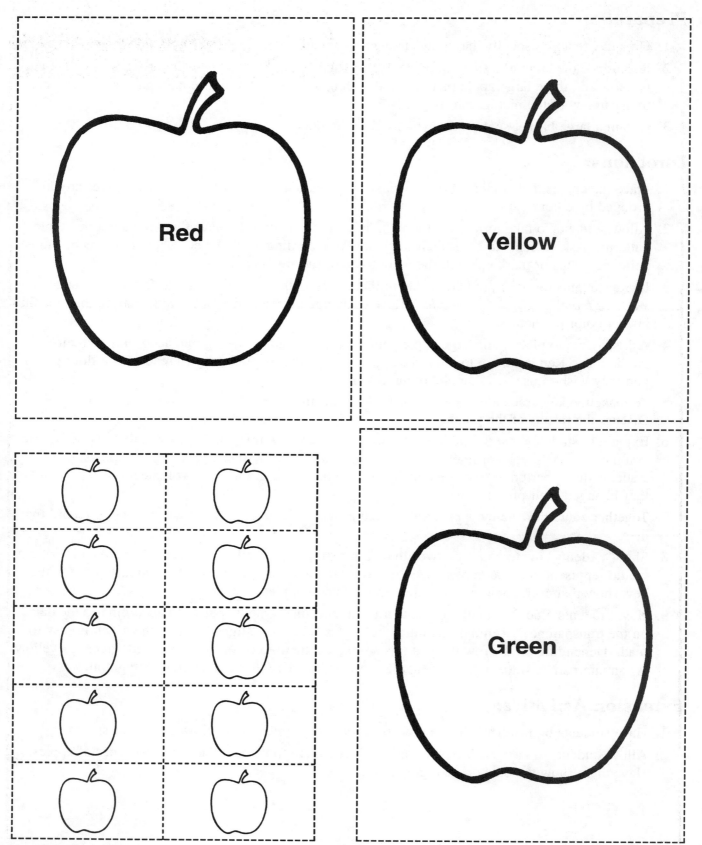

Apples *(cont.)*

APPLES	
Red	
Yellow	
Green	

Key: 1 🍎 = _____

Teeth

You may wish to use this graphing activity as part of a dental health unit.

Preparation:

1. Reproduce the table (page 6) and the pictograph (page 18) for students and make overhead transparencies of these pages.

2. Make an overhead transparency of the Teeth Diagram (page 17). You may also wish to reproduce this for students.

3. Reproduce the large and small tooth patterns (page 17) and the pictograph (page 18).

Directions:

1. Give each student one large tooth pattern and about 20 small tooth patterns.

2. Show the Teeth Diagram. Discuss the names of the teeth and the difference between baby teeth and permanent teeth.

3. Ask students to count how many baby teeth they have lost. Have them raise their hands as you call out each number of teeth lost. Point out that 4+ means that 4 or more baby teeth have been lost. Use the overhead transparency to record the data, as shown in the example below. Ask students to record the data on their copies of the table.

LOST TEETH	
Number of Teeth Lost	**Number of Students**
0	0
1	3
2	6
3	4
4 +	5

4. Use the floor or wall graph to model the activity. Trace a large tooth pattern to make the key: 1 Tooth = 1 Student. Tell students to write their names on the large tooth patterns. Have them place these in the appropriate sections of the graph, making sure they are aligned vertically.

5. Review with students how to count by twos to compress the data. Remind them that half of a tooth pattern would represent one student who has lost that number of teeth. Use the transparency of the pictograph to demonstrate. On the key, show that each tooth pattern represents two students.

6. Invite students to glue the small patterns on their pictographs (page 18) according to the data. Remind them that the teeth should be aligned so that the graph is easy to read.

7. Discuss the questions (page 18) and ask additional ones to check students' understanding.

Extension Activities:

1. Make arrangements to have a local dentist visit your classroom.

2. Review how students should brush their teeth. Then have them keep a daily log to show when they brush their teeth.

Teeth *(cont.)*

Teeth Diagram

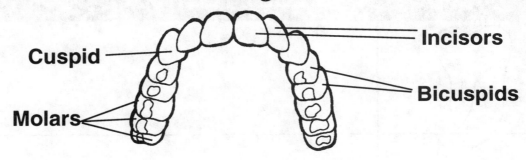

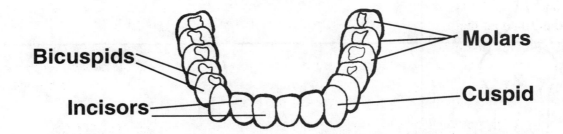

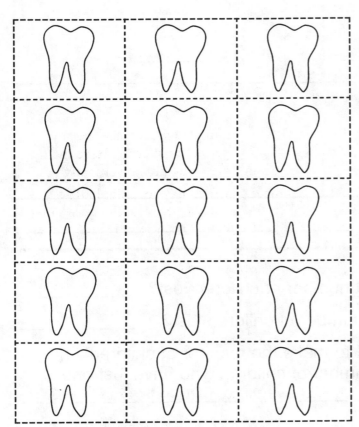

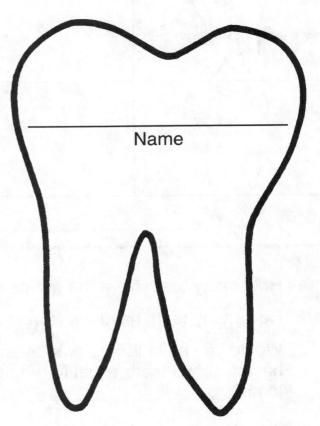

Name

Teeth *(cont.)*

LOST TEETH	
0	
1	
2	
3	
4+	

Key: 1 ⬜ = _____

1. How many teeth have the greatest number of children lost? _____

2. How many teeth have the fewest number of children lost? _____

3. Would you have to add or subtract to make the number of children who have lost two teeth equal to the number of children who have lost one tooth? _____

Ice Cream

Preparation:

1. Reproduce the table (page 6) and pictograph (page 21) for students and make overhead transparencies of these pages.
2. Reproduce the large and small ice cream cone patterns (page 20). Give each student one large ice cream cone and about 20 small ice cream cones.

Directions:

1. Have students cut apart the patterns. Allow them to decorate their large ice cream cones using crayons or markers.
2. One at a time, have students place their large ice cream cones on the wall or floor graph next to their favorite flavors. Use a large ice cream cone pattern to make the key, showing that one ice cream cone represents one vote.
3. Show students how to count by twos to compress the data. Point out that half of an ice cream cone would represent one vote. Use the transparency of the pictograph to demonstrate.
   Examples: *If six students voted for chocolate, you would draw three ice cream cones. If five students voted for chocolate, you would draw two and one-half ice cream cones.* On the key, show that each ice cream cone represents two votes.
4. Use the overhead transparency of the table to record the data from the wall or floor graph. See the example below. Have students record the data on their copies of the table.

OUR FAVORITE ICE CREAM FLAVORS	
Ice Cream Flavors	**Number of Votes**
Chocolate	9
Vanilla	8
Strawberry	3

5. Have students arrange the small ice cream cones on their pictographs (page 21), according to the data provided by the class. After checking the graphs for accuracy, have students adhere their pictures with glue.
6. Discuss the questions (page 21) and ask additional ones to check students' understanding.

Extension Activities:

1. Use ice cream stickers (TCM 1348) to create the pictograph.
2. Have students use an ice cream maker to prepare some homemade ice cream. Be sure to ask parents if their children have any food allergies or dietary restrictions.
3. Divide the class into small groups. Have each group brainstorm a list of ice cream flavors. Have a contest to see which group can list the greatest number of flavors.
4. Have students do research to learn about the invention of ice cream.
5. Encourage students to make advertisements for new flavors or combinations of ice creams.

Ice Cream *(cont.)*

20

Ice Cream *(cont.)*

OUR FAVORITE ICE CREAM FLAVORS

Chocolate	
Vanilla	
Strawberry	

Key: 1 🍦 = _____

1. What is the title of the graph? _____

   _____

2. Which flavors of ice cream does the graph show? _____

   _____

3. What does the key tell you? _____

   _____

4. How many children like chocolate the most? _____ vanilla? _____
   strawberry? _____

5. Do more children like chocolate or vanilla?_____

6. Do more children like vanilla or strawberry? _____

Shoes

Preparation:

1. Reproduce the table (page 6) and pictograph (page 24) for students and make overhead transparencies of these pages.
2. Reproduce the large and small shoe patterns (page 23).

Directions:

1. Begin by having students look at their own shoes as well as those of nearby classmates. Discuss the different types of shoes people wear. Tell students to determine if they are wearing shoes that tie, have straps with Velcro®, tie and have Velcro® straps, or slip on or buckle.
2. Divide the class into four groups according to the types of shoes they are wearing.
3. Encourage students to help you count the number of students in each group. Use the overhead transparency to record the data, as shown in the example below. Have students record the data on their copies of the table.

SHOES	
Types of Shoes	**Number of Students**
Tie	13
Velcro®	4
Tie + Velcro®	6
Slip On or Buckle	2

4. Use the floor or wall graph to model the activity. Cut out and trace the outline of a large shoe pattern to make the key: 1 Shoe = 1 Student.
5. Distribute the large shoe patterns to each group, matching the pattern to the type of shoes students are wearing. For example, the group of students who are wearing shoes that tie should be given patterns of shoes that tie.
6. Invite students to place their large shoe patterns in the appropriate rows on the graph. Help them make sure the patterns are properly aligned.
7. Review with students how to count by twos to compress the data. Remind them that half of a shoe pattern would represent one student who is wearing that type of shoes. Use the transparency of the pictograph to demonstrate. On the key, show that each shoe pattern represents two students.
8. Invite students to glue the small shoe patterns on their pictographs (page 24) according to the data. Remind them that the shoes should be aligned so that the graph is easy to read.
9. Discuss the questions (page 24) and ask additional ones to check students' understanding.

Extension Activities:

1. For homework, have students create pictographs that show what kinds of shoes their families have.
2. Invite each student to design his or her own pair of shoes. Ask them to draw diagrams and label the parts of their new shoes.

Shoes *(cont.)*

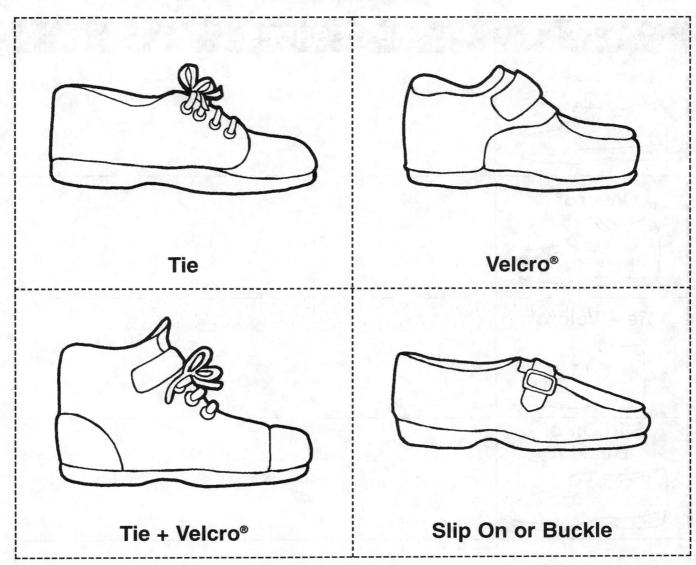

Tie

Velcro®

Tie + Velcro®

Slip On or Buckle

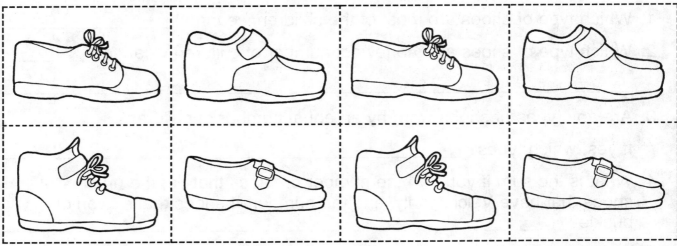

Shoes *(cont.)*

TYPES OF SHOES	
Tie	
Velcro®	
Tie + Velcro®	
Slip On or Buckle	
Key: 1 = _____	

1. Which type of shoes are most of the children wearing? _____

2. Which type of shoes are the fewest number of children wearing? _____

   _____

3. Are any types of shoes worn by an equal number of children? _____

   If yes, which types? _____

4. What is the sum if you add the number of shoes that tie, the number of shoes that have Velcro® only, and the number of shoes that slip on or buckle? _____

Fruit

Preparation:

1. Reproduce the table (page 6) and pictograph (page 27) for students and make overhead transparencies of these pages.

2. Reproduce the large and small fruit patterns (page 26). Give each student several copies of each type of small pattern.

3. Obtain apples, oranges, and bananas for students to eat. You may wish to cut each piece of fruit in half. Be sure to ask parents if their children have any food allergies or dietary restrictions.

Directions:

1. Ask each student to choose her/his favorite type of fruit for snack and provide a large fruit pattern that matches. Record students' choices on the transparency of the table. See the example below. Allow students to eat their fruit while they record the data on their copies of the table.

OUR FAVORITE FRUIT	
Type of Fruit	**Number of Votes**
Orange	7
Banana	7
Apple	10

2. Use the floor or wall graph to model the activity. One at a time, have students place their large patterns on the graph next to their favorite fruits. Help them vertically align the patterns to ensure that the graph is easy to read. Make the key: 1 Fruit = 1 Vote.

3. Show students how to count by twos to compress the data. Point out that half of any fruit pattern represents one vote. Use the transparency of the pictograph to demonstrate. On the key, show that each fruit represents two votes.

4. Have students arrange the small fruit patterns on their pictographs (page 27) according to the data. After checking the graphs for accuracy and alignment, have students adhere their pictures with glue.

5. Discuss the questions (page 27) and ask additional ones to check students' understanding. Have students practice basic addition and subtraction facts by asking: *How many votes would you have to add to the _____ (second most liked fruit) to make the number equal to the number of votes for the _____ (most liked)? How many votes would you have to take away from the _____ (most liked fruit) to make the number equal to the number of votes for the _____ (least liked)?*

Extension Activities:

1. Invite small groups to make collages, using pictures of fruits from magazines and newspapers.

2. Give each pair of students a balance scale, apple, orange, and banana. Have the partners use the scale to determine which piece of fruit weighs the most and which weighs the least. Ask them to arrange their pieces of fruit by weight in order from greatest to least.

Fruit (cont.)

Apple

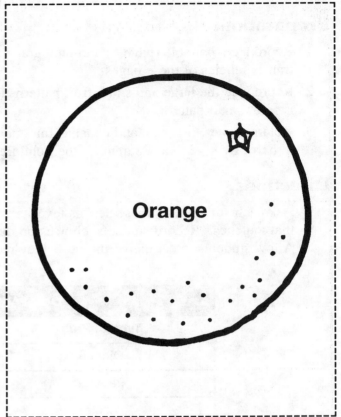

Orange

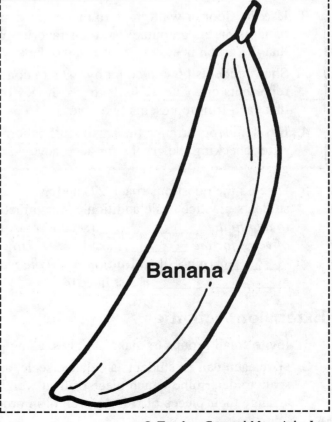

Banana

Fruit *(cont.)*

OUR FAVORITE FRUIT

Apple	
Orange	
Banana	

Key: 1 Fruit = _____

1. Which type of fruit is liked the most? _____

2. Which type of fruit is liked the least? _____

3. How many children like apples best?_____
   bananas? _____ oranges?_____

4. Would you have to add or subtract to make the number of votes for apples equal to the number of votes for oranges? _____

5. If twice as many children had voted for bananas, how many children would have liked bananas the most? _____

Pockets

Preparation:

1. Reproduce the table (page 6) for students and make an overhead transparency of it.
2. Reproduce the large and small pocket patterns (page 29) and the pictograph (page 30).
3. Obtain a copy of the book *Katy No-Pocket* by Emmy Payne (Houghton Mifflin, 1944).

Directions:

1. Begin this activity by reading aloud *Katy No-Pocket*. Discuss kangaroos. Point out that mother kangaroos really do have pockets for their babies. Talk about the man in the story who has lots of pockets. Have students suggest uses for pockets for people and animals.
2. Have students help you count how many pockets there are in your clothes.
3. Distribute the large pocket patterns, one per student. Ask students to write their names on the patterns. Assign partners. Have students help each other count how many pockets they have. Tell them to write the number of pockets they have on their patterns.
4. Use the floor or wall graph to model the activity. To make the key, trace a large pocket pattern and show that each pattern represents a student who has that number of pockets. Point out that 4+ means that there are 4 or more pockets in the clothing a student is wearing.
5. Allow students to place their large pocket patterns in the appropriate sections of the graph, making sure they are aligned vertically.
6. Have students use the graph to help you count how many students have each number of pockets. Use the overhead transparency to record the data, as shown in the example below. Ask students to record the data on their copies of the table.

POCKETS	
Number of Pockets	**Number of Students**
0	1
1	4
2	7
3	4
4 +	3

7. Provide copies of the small pocket patterns and ask students to cut them out. Students do not need to write anything on these. Have them use the data on their tables and the small pocket patterns to create their pictographs. Remind them to align the pockets. They may wish to use differently colored crayons or markers to help differentiate the pockets on each row of the graph.
8. Discuss the questions (page 30) and ask additional ones to check students' understanding.

Extension Activities:

1. Encourage students to learn more about kangaroos.
2. Have students create a graph that shows how many pockets the class has each day for a week.
3. Have students sort pictures of clothes into groups according to the number of pockets.

Pockets *(cont.)*

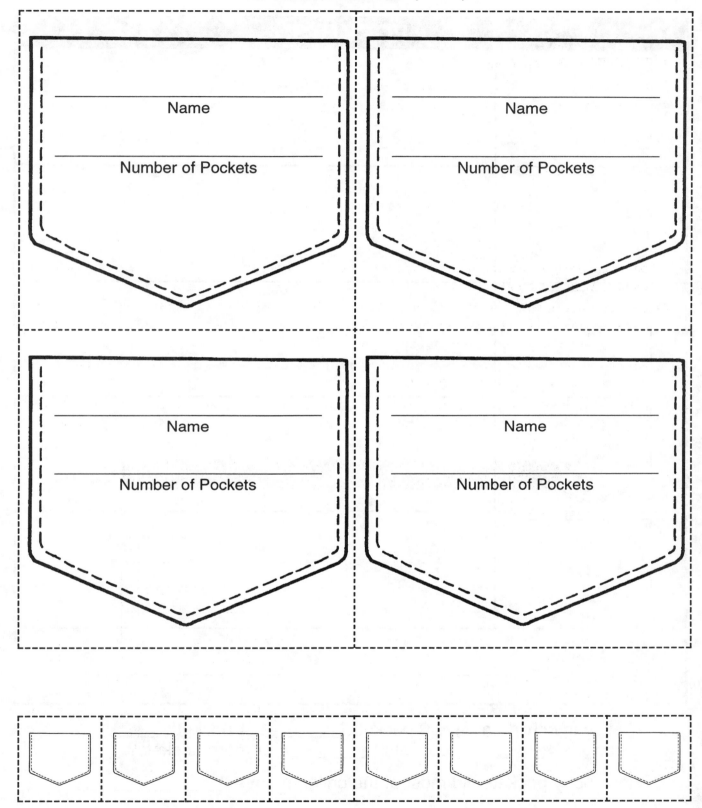

_____
Name

_____
Number of Pockets

_____
Name

_____
Number of Pockets

_____
Name

_____
Number of Pockets

_____
Name

_____
Number of Pockets

Pockets *(cont.)*

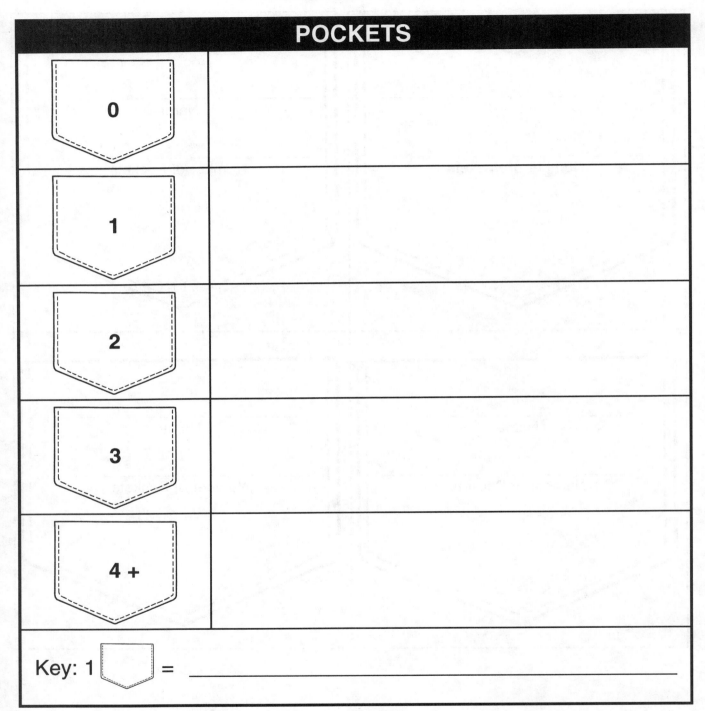

POCKETS	
0	
1	
2	
3	
4 +	

Key: 1 ⬖ = _____

1. How many children have 0 pockets?_____ 1 pocket?_____
   2 pockets? _____ 3 pockets? _____ 4 or more pockets? _____

2. How many pockets did most of the children have? _____

3. How many children have 1 or more pockets in their clothes? _____

Birthdays

Preparation:

1. Reproduce the table (page 6) for students and make two overhead transparencies of it.
2. Enlarge the calendar circle (page 32) on poster board or make an overhead transparency of it.
3. Reproduce the patterns (page 32) so that each student gets one large birthday cake, enough candles to show his/her age, and about 20 small birthday cakes.
4. Reproduce the pictograph (page 33).

Directions:

1. Ask each student to sign her/his name on the calendar circle to show in which month she/he was born. Encourage the class to help you count the number of students who have birthdays during each month. Use the overhead transparency of the table to record the data, as shown below. Ask students to record the data on their copies of the table.

BIRTHDAYS	
Month	**Number of Students**
January	1
February	2
March	2
April	3
May	0
June	3
July	1
August	1
September	2
October	4
November	3
December	2

2. Use the floor or wall graph to model the activity. To make the key, use a large birthday cake pattern to show that each cake represents one student who has a birthday during that month.
3. Provide each student with a large birthday cake pattern and enough candles to show her/his age. Ask students to glue the candles onto their cakes. Have students place the large cakes in the appropriate sections of the graph, making sure they are aligned vertically.
4. Have students use the data and the small cake patterns to create their pictographs. Remind them to align the cakes. Encourage students to count by twos to compress the data.
5. Ask students questions about the graph to check their understanding.

Extension Activities:

1. Have each student write the day of her/his birth on a large cake pattern. Ask students to help you arrange the cakes in numerical order for each month on the wall or floor graph.
2. Teach students the abbreviations for the months of the year.
3. Ask students to make graphs that show the months in which their family members were born.

Birthdays *(cont.)*

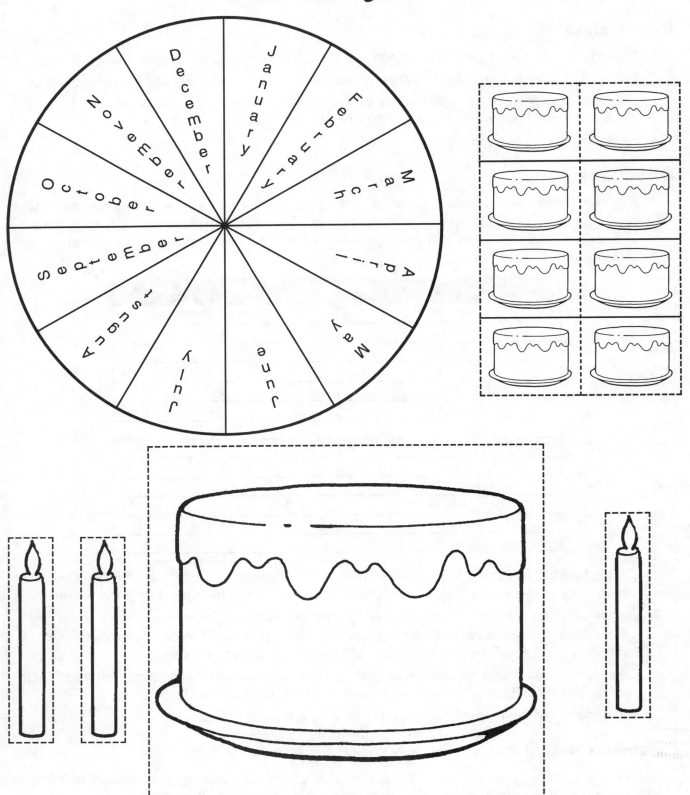

Birthdays *(cont.)*

BIRTHDAYS	
January	
February	
March	
April	
May	
June	
July	
August	
September	
October	
November	
December	

Key: 1 🎂 = _____

Boys and Girls

Preparation:

1. Make overhead transparencies of the table (page 6) and the pictograph (page 36). You may need more than one copy of the table, depending on the number of students you have in your class.

2. Reproduce the large and small boy and girl patterns (page 35) and the pictograph (page 36).

Directions:

1. Give a large boy pattern to each boy and a large girl pattern to each girl. Ask students to write their names on the patterns.

2. Encourage students to color the patterns to look like them.

3. One at a time, invite students to sign their names under the appropriate heading on the transparency of the table. After everyone has signed, have students help you count the number of boys and girls in each column. Record those numbers next to the headings as shown in the following example.

BOYS AND GIRLS	
Boys 12	**Girls 9**
Joseph	Kristin
Andreas	LaShanda
Mike	Nikki
Tyrone	Maria

4. Use the floor or wall graph to model the activity. Make the key: 1 Picture = 1 boy or girl. Have students place their large boy and girl patterns in the appropriate sections of the graph, making sure they are aligned vertically.

5. Show students how to count by twos to compress the data. Point out that half of a pattern represents one child. Use the transparency of the pictograph to demonstrate. On the key, show that each picture represents two boys/girls.

6. Distribute the small boy and girl patterns. Have students use the data on the transparency and the small boy and girl patterns to create their pictographs. After checking the graphs for accuracy and alignment, have students glue their pictures in place.

7. Discuss the questions (page 36) and ask additional ones to check students' understanding.

Extension Activities:

1. Ask students to create a wall graph of boys and girls, using photographs of themselves.

2. Have students name words that have the same vowel sound as *boy*. **Examples:** *boil, broil, toy, joy, join, coin.* Then have them name words that have the same vowel sound as *girl*. **Examples:** *curl, dirt, earth, first, germ, hurt, learn, pearl, sir, turn, verb, word.*

3. Have students make graphs to show the number of boys and girls in your grade level or in the entire school.

4. Allow students to cut and paste magazine and newspaper pictures to make two collages, one of boys and the other of girls.

Boys and Girls (cont.)

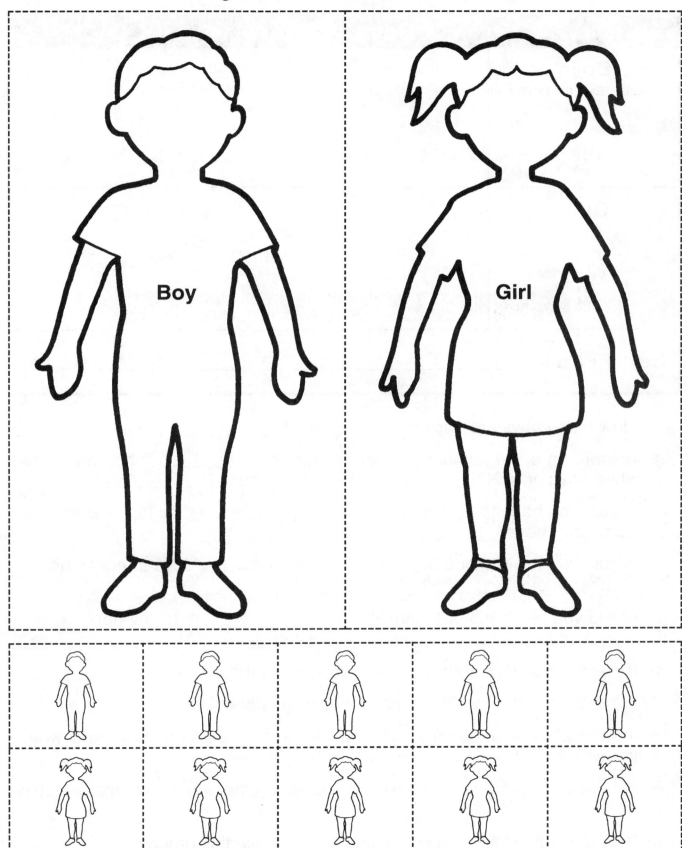

Boys and Girls *(cont.)*

	Boys + Girls
Boys	
Girls	

Key: 1 Picture = _____

1. How many boys are shown on this graph? _____ girls? _____

2. Is there an equal number of boys and girls? _____ If not, are there more boys or girls? _____ How many more? _____

3. Would you have to add or subtract for the number of girls to equal the number of boys?_____

4. Would you have to add or subtract for the number of boys to equal the number of girls? _____

5. Could you pair each boy with a girl? _____ If not, why not?

   _____

6. If there were 10 more boys, how many would there be?_____

7. If there were 10 more girls, how many would there be? _____

8. If there were twice as many boys as shown on the graph, how many would there be? _____

9. If there were twice as many girls as shown on the graph, how many would there be? _____

10. How many boys and girls were counted to make this graph?_____

Buttons

Preparation:

1. Obtain a copy of the book *Corduroy* by Don Freeman (Viking, 1968).
2. Reproduce the table (page 6), large button patterns (page 38), and bar graph (page 39) for students. Make an overhead transparency of the table.

Directions:

1. Begin this activity by reading *Corduroy*. Discuss the story with students. Point out that Corduroy lost a button.
2. Show examples of buttons on students' clothing as well as on your own. Have students help you count the buttons on your clothes.
3. Distribute the large button patterns, one per student. Assign partners. Have students help each other count how many buttons they have. Tell them to write the number of buttons they have on their patterns.
4. Use the floor or wall graph to model the activity. Mark the scale on the left-hand side: 0, 1–2, 3–4, 5–6, 7+. Point out the range of this scale. Review how 7+ means that there are seven or more buttons on the clothing a student is wearing. Then show students how to mark the scale along the bottom, counting by ones or twos.
5. Help students place the bars on the graph.
6. Have students use the graph to count how many students have each number of buttons. Use the overhead transparency to record the data, as shown in the example below. Ask students to record the data on their copies of the table.

BUTTONS ON OUR CLOTHES	
Number of Buttons	Number of Students
0	1
1–2	4
3–4	7
5–6	4
7+	4

7. Have students color the bar graphs according to the data on their tables.
8. Discuss the questions (page 39) and ask additional ones to check students' understanding.

Extension Activities:

1. Create pictographs, using the small button patterns (page 38).
2. Provide each pair of students with a variety of buttons in a reclosable plastic bag. Ask students to sort the buttons into groups. They may choose to sort them by color, size, shape, the number of holes, etc.
3. Have students use buttons to create patterns. Ask them to tell the class about their patterns.
4. Encourage students to bring spare buttons from home. Ask them to glue their buttons together to make imaginary creatures. Allow time for students to tell about their button animals.

Buttons *(cont.)*

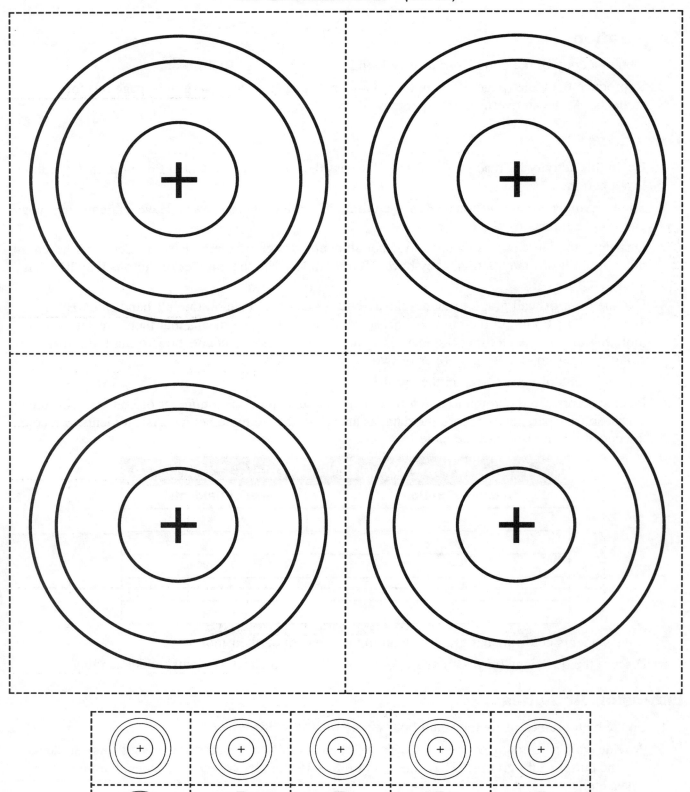

38

Buttons (cont.)

BUTTONS ON OUR CLOTHES

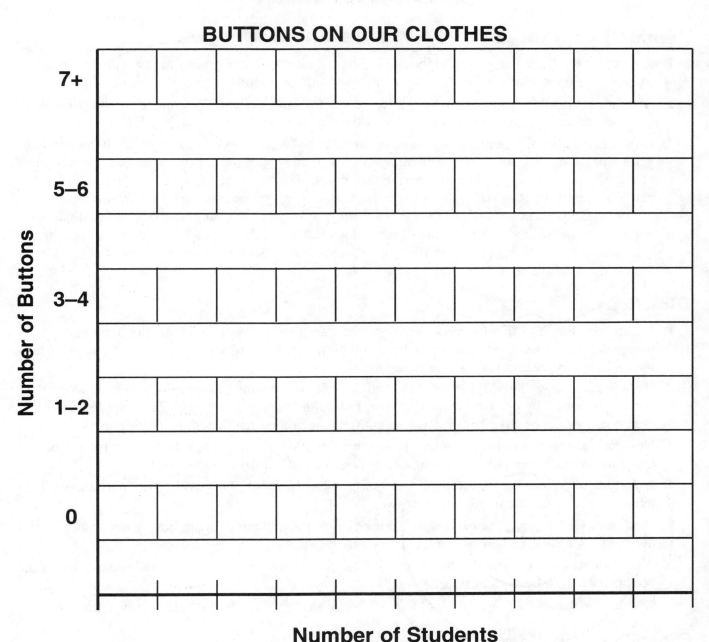

1. What is the title of this graph? _____

2. How many children have 0 buttons? _____
   1 or 2 buttons? _____   3 or 4 buttons? _____
   5 or 6 buttons? _____   7 or more buttons? _____

3. How many buttons are most of the children wearing? _____

4. How many buttons are the least number of children wearing? _____

5. How many children have one or more buttons on their clothes? _____

Pasta

Preparation:

1. Reproduce the three bar graphs (pages 43–45) for students. Three graphs are provided to give students the opportunity to sort pasta patterns by color, size, and type.

2. Reproduce the table (page 6), making three copies for each student. You may also wish to make an overhead transparency of it to model how the data is recorded for each graph activity.

3. Reproduce the small, medium, and large pasta patterns (pages 41 and 42) on green, blue, red, and yellow paper or cardstock and cut them apart. Make one set of pasta patterns for each small group or pair of students. The number of each color, size, and type of pasta can vary. Place the patterns in envelopes or reclosable plastic bags, making all of the sets exactly the same. If you prefer, students can use real pasta for these sorting activities. To change the color of real pasta, place 15 drops of food coloring and 2 tablespoons (30 mL) rubbing alcohol in a container with a lid. Shake the container. Remove the colored pasta and allow it to dry. The amount of food color affects the brightness of the color.

Directions:

1. Divide the class into small groups or assign partners. First have students sort the pasta into groups by color. Ask them to count how many pasta pieces there are for each color (green, blue, red, yellow) and record the data on their tables.

2. Use the floor or wall graph to model the activity. Show students how to mark the scale along the bottom, counting by ones or twos. Help them place the bars on the graph. Then ask them to record the results on their bar graphs (page 43), using colors that match the pasta groups.

3. Next have students sort the pasta into groups by size. Ask them to count how many pasta pieces there are for each size (small, medium, large) and record the data on their tables.

4. Ask students to record the results on their bar graphs (page 44). Discuss how to mark the scale on the left-hand side, counting by ones or twos.

5. Now have students sort the pasta into groups by type. Ask them to count how many pasta pieces there are for each type and record the data on their tables.

6. Ask students to record the results on their bar graphs. Show them how to mark the scale along the bottom, counting by ones or twos.

7. Discuss the questions (pages 43–45) and ask additional ones to check students' understanding.

Extension Activities:

1. Teach students about probability, using the pasta patterns. After determining the number of each color, size, and type of pasta, have students replace the patterns in the bags or envelopes. Then have students make predictions about which color, size, and/or type of pasta is most or least likely to be drawn or which ones have an equal chance.

2. Create pictographs, using the pasta patterns (pages 41 and 42).

3. Have students make pasta salad for snack. Be sure to ask parents if their children have any food allergies or dietary restrictions.

Pasta *(cont.)*

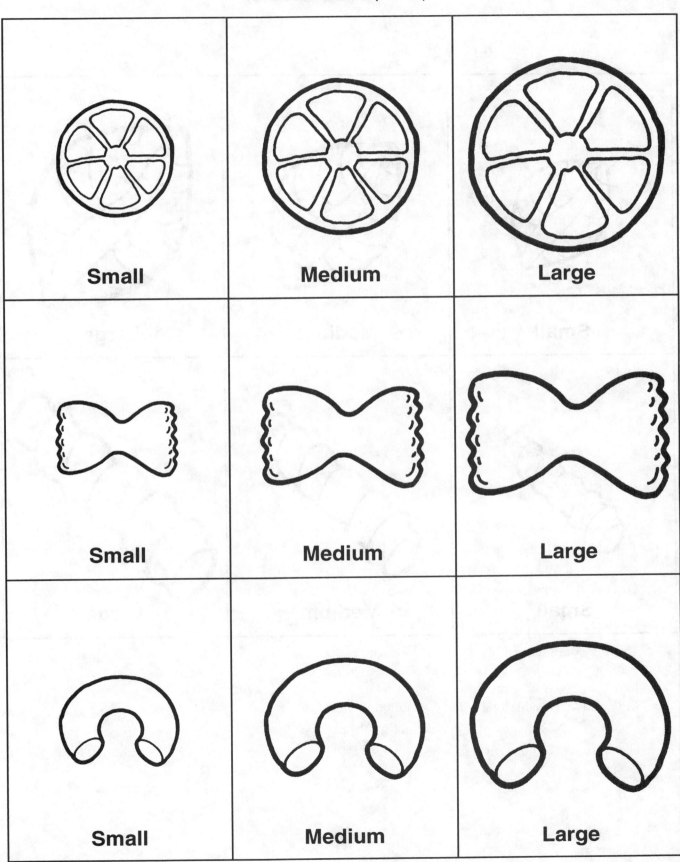

| Small | Medium | Large |

| Small | Medium | Large |

| Small | Medium | Large |

Pasta *(cont.)*

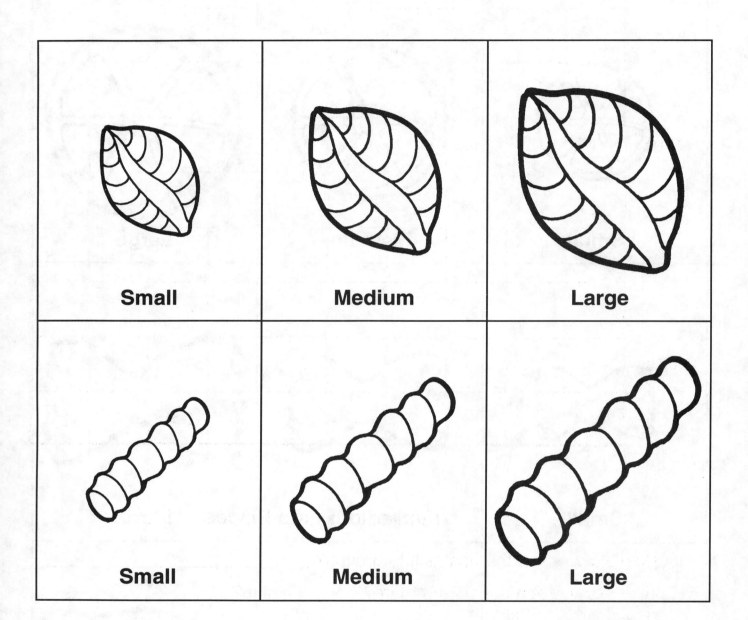

Small	Medium	Large

Small	Medium	Large

42

Pasta *(cont.)*

PASTA COLORS

Green

Blue

Red

Yellow

Number of Pasta Pieces

1. How did you sort the pastas into groups? _____

2. How many green pastas are there? _____ blue? _____ red? _____ yellow? _____

3. Which color of pasta has the most? _____ Which color has the least? _____

4. Is the number of green pastas greater than, less than, or equal to the number of red pastas? _____

5. Is the number of yellow pastas greater than, less than, or equal to the number of blue pastas? _____

Pasta *(cont.)*

PASTA SIZES

Number of Pasta Pieces

Large　　　**Medium**　　　**Small**

1. How did you sort the pastas into groups? _____

2. How many large pastas are there? _____
   medium? _____ small?_____

3. Which size pasta has the most? _____ Which size has the
   least?_____

4. How many pieces of large and medium pastas are there all together? _____

5. Would you have to add or subtract to make the number of small pastas
   equal to the number of large pastas? _____

Pasta *(cont.)*

TYPES OF PASTA

Number of Pasta Pieces

1. How did you sort the pastas into groups? _____

2. How many groups of pasta are there?_____

3. How many pieces are in the largest group of pasta? _____

4. How many pieces are in the smallest group of pasta? _____

5. If you combine the largest group and the smallest group of pasta, how many pieces will you have? _____

Peanut Butter and Jelly

Preparation:

1. Reproduce the table (page 6) for students and make an overhead transparency of it.
2. Reproduce the bar graph (page 48) for students.
3. Purchase peanut butter, jelly, and bread to make sandwiches. For students who do not like peanut butter or jelly, you may wish to provide an alternative such as cheese sandwiches. Be sure to ask parents if their children have any food allergies or dietary restrictions.

Directions:

1. Discuss how a peanut butter and jelly sandwich is made. Explain that people like their sandwiches made different ways. Some like peanut butter with jelly, while others like peanut butter without jelly. Some like jelly but not peanut butter. Others do not like peanut butter or jelly.
2. Provide a dull knife, paper plates or paper towels, bread, jelly, and peanut butter. Ask each student to make a sandwich the way that she/he likes it best. Record students' choices on the transparency of the table, as shown in the example below. Allow students to eat their sandwiches as they record the data on their copies of the table.

PEANUT BUTTER AND JELLY	
Type of Sandwich	**Number of Votes**
Peanut Butter	8
Jelly	4
Peanut Butter with Jelly	10
No Peanut Butter or Jelly	1

3. Use the floor or wall graph to model the activity. Show students how to mark the scale on the left-hand side, counting by ones or twos. Help students place the bars on the graph.
4. Have students record the results on their bar graphs.
5. Discuss the questions (page 48) and ask additional ones to check students' understanding. Have students practice basic addition and subtraction facts by asking: *How many votes would you have to add to the _____ sandwiches (second most liked) to make the number equal to the _____ sandwiches (most liked)? How many votes would you have to take away from the _____ sandwiches (most liked) to make the number equal to the _____ sandwiches (least liked)?*

Extension Activities:

1. Have students work together to tell how to make a peanut butter sandwich. Be sure they put the steps in the correct order.
2. Create pictographs, using the sandwich patterns (page 47).
3. Have students follow a recipe to make homemade peanut butter. Allow them to taste it.
4. Read aloud the book *Peanut Butter and Jelly* by Nadine Bernard Westcott (Dutton, 1987).

Peanut Butter and Jelly *(cont.)*

Peanut Buttter

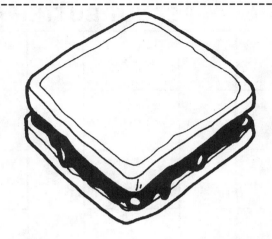

Jelly

Peanut Butter with Jelly

No Peanut Butter or Jelly

Peanut Butter

Jelly

Peanut Butter with Jelly

No Peanut Butter or Jelly

Peanut Butter

Jelly

Peanut Butter with Jelly

No Peanut Butter or Jelly

Peanut Butter and Jelly *(cont.)*

PEANUT BUTTER AND JELLY SANDWICHES

Number of Votes

| Peanut Butter | Jelly | Peanut Butter with Jelly | No Peanut Butter or Jelly |

1. Which type of sandwich is liked the most? _____

2. Which type of sandwich is liked the least? _____

3. How many children like peanut butter sandwiches? _____
jelly sandwiches? _____ peanut butter with jelly sandwiches? _____

4. How many children do not like peanut butter or jelly sandwiches? _____

5. Are any of the sandwiches liked by an equal number of children? _____
If yes, which ones? _____

Families

Preparation:

1. Reproduce the table (page 6) and make an overhead transparency of it.
2. Reproduce the bar graph (page 50) for students.

Directions:

1. Discuss what a family is and why it is important.
2. Ask five volunteers to tell how many family members they have. Students may wish to include siblings or parents who do not live with them as well as grandparents or other relatives who do live with them. Record students' responses on the transparency of the table, as shown below.

OUR FAMILIES	
Student	**Number of Family Members**
Mack	3
Shavone	4
Phillip	7
Brenda	2
Antonio	3

3. Use the floor or wall graph to model the activity. Show students how to mark the scale on the left-hand side, counting by ones or twos. Help students place the bars on the graph.
4. Allow students to ask how many family members any five of their classmates have. If you prefer to use this activity as a homework assignment, tell students to ask how many family members five of their friends have. This way they can use information from people who are not in the same class. Tell students to record the data on their copies of the table.
5. Have students record the results on their bar graphs.
6. Discuss the questions (page 50) and ask additional ones to check students' understanding.
7. You may wish to ask students to tell the class about their graphs.

Extension Activities:

1. Allow students to interview teachers or students in another class to determine how many family members each person has. Help students use this data to create bar graphs.
2. Have students write stories about a family tradition. Encourage them to share their stories with the class.
3. Ask parents to help their children create a family tree that includes as many family members as possible.
4. Have students bring photographs of their families. Use these to create a class pictograph.
5. Read aloud some literature about families. Try to include stories about families from around the world.
6. Have students dictate or write letters to their families, telling them why they are special. Encourage students to give the letters to their families.

Families (cont.)

OUR FAMILIES

Number of Family Members

Names

1. Who has the largest family? _____

2. Who has the smallest family? _____

3. Do any of the people have families that are the same size?_____
   If yes, which ones? _____

4. If you combine all of these families, how many people are there all
   together? _____

5. How many more family members does the largest family have than the
   smallest family? _____

Eye Color

Preparation:

1. Reproduce the table (page 6) and make an overhead transparency of it.

2. Reproduce the large eye patterns (page 52) and the bar graph (page 53) for students. Cut apart the eye patterns but do not color them.

3. Obtain small hand-held mirrors for students to use. You may wish to have small groups of students share the mirrors to reduce the number needed.

Directions:

1. Begin this activity by discussing the similarities and differences among people's appearances. Point out what color your eyes are and explain that your eye color might be similar to some students but different from others.

2. Provide mirrors for students to determine their eye colors. Have them tell you what color their eyes are. If necessary, help them identify their eye colors. Distribute the eye patterns according to students' eye colors. Ask students to color the patterns the same colors as their eyes. If a student has blue-green or hazel eyes, he or she can choose either blue or green, or you can substitute blue-green or hazel for gray on the table, eye pattern, and graph.

3. As you call each color (brown, blue, green, gray) listed on the table, have students raise their eye patterns if their eyes are that color. Invite the class to help you count the eye patterns to determine how many students have each eye color. Record the data on the transparency of the table, as shown in the example below. Have students write the data on their copies of the table.

EYE COLORS	
Color of Eyes	**Number of Students**
Brown	12
Blue	8
Green	2
Gray	0

4. Use the floor or wall graph to model the activity. Show students how to mark the scale along the bottom, counting by ones, twos, or threes. Help students place the bars on the graph.

5. Have students record the results on their bar graphs.

6. Discuss the questions (page 53) and ask additional ones to check students' understanding.

Extension Activities:

1. Explain that the pupil is the black circle that is in the center of each eye. Point out that the pupil changes size to allow more or less light into the eye. The more light there is, the smaller the pupil gets. The less light there is, the larger the pupil gets. Assign partners or provide a mirror for each student. Turn off the lights for a couple of minutes. Ask students to observe the changes in the pupils.

2. Create pictographs, using the small eye patterns (page 52).

3. Invite students to name objects in the classroom that are the same colors as their eyes.

Eye Color *(cont.)*

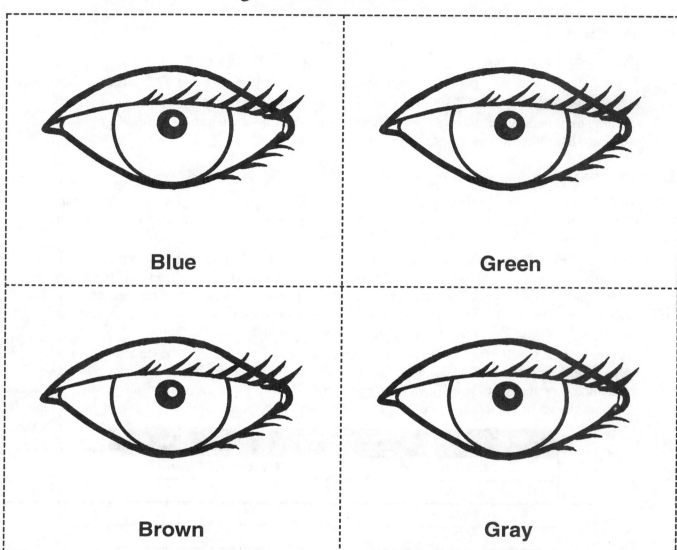

Blue

Green

Brown

Gray

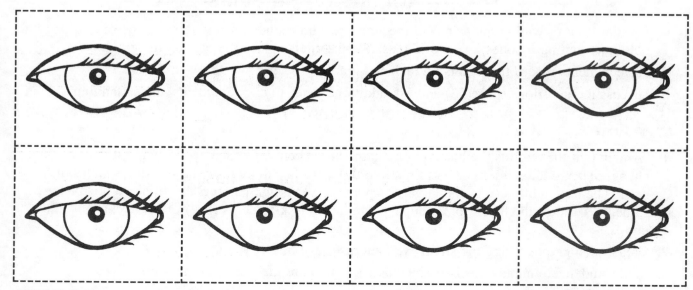

Eye Color *(cont.)*

OUR EYE COLORS

Number of Students

1. Which eye color do most of the children have? _____

2. Which eye color do the fewest number of children have? _____

3. Are any of the eye colors equal in number? _____ If yes, which colors?

   _____

4. How many would you have to subtract from the most common eye color to make it equal to the second most common eye color? _____

5. Would you have to add or subtract to make the number of children with blue eyes equal to the number of children with brown eyes? _____

Hair Color

Preparation:

1. Reproduce the table (page 6) and make an overhead transparency of it.
2. Reproduce the hair patterns (page 55) and the bar graph (page 56) for students. Cut apart the hair patterns but do not color them.
3. Obtain small hand-held mirrors for students to use. You may wish to have small groups of students share the mirrors to reduce the number needed.

Directions:

1. Point out what color your hair is and explain that your hair color might be similar to some students but different from others.
2. Provide mirrors for students to determine their hair colors. Have them tell you what color their hair is. If necessary, help them identify their hair colors. Distribute the boy hair patterns to the boys according to their hair colors. Then do the same for the girls, gives the girl hair patterns. Ask students to color the patterns the same colors as their hair. If a student has a hair color different from the choices provided, you can combine that color with black on the table and graph. Substitute that color on one of the hair patterns.
3. As you call each color (brown, blonde, red, black) listed on the table, have students raise their hair patterns if their hair is that color. Invite the class to help you count the hair patterns to determine how many students have each hair color. Record the data on the transparency of the table, as shown in the example below. Have students write the data on their copies of the table.

HAIR COLOR	
Colors of Hair	**Number of Students**
Brown	15
Blond	4
Red	0
Black	1

4. Use the floor or wall graph to model the activity. Show students how to mark the scale on the left-hand side, counting by ones, twos, or threes. Help students place the bars on the graph.
5. Have students record the results on their bar graphs.
6. Discuss the questions (page 56) and ask additional ones to check students' understanding.

Extension Activities:

1. Have students make bar graphs that show how many students have curly and straight hair.
2. Invite pairs of students to determine how many combinations of hair color (brown, blonde, red, black) and eye color (blue, brown, green, gray) they can name. Examples: *blue eyes with brown hair, blue eyes with blonde hair, blue eyes with red hair, blue eyes with black hair.*
3. Ask students to create paper-plate faces that look like them. Tell them to color the eyes the same color as their own eyes and use yarn that approximately matches the color of their hair.

Hair Color *(cont.)*

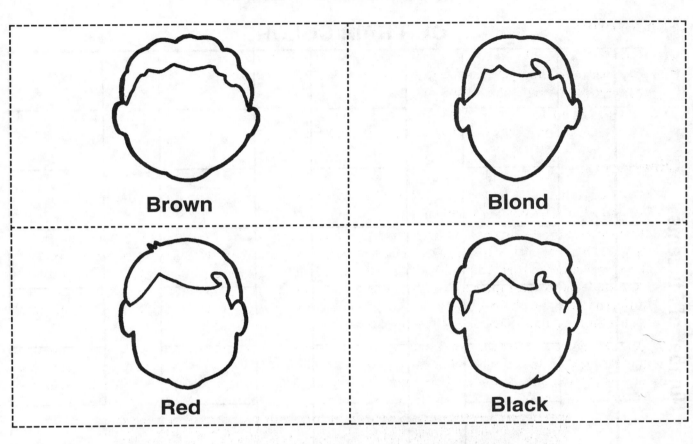

Brown

Blond

Red

Black

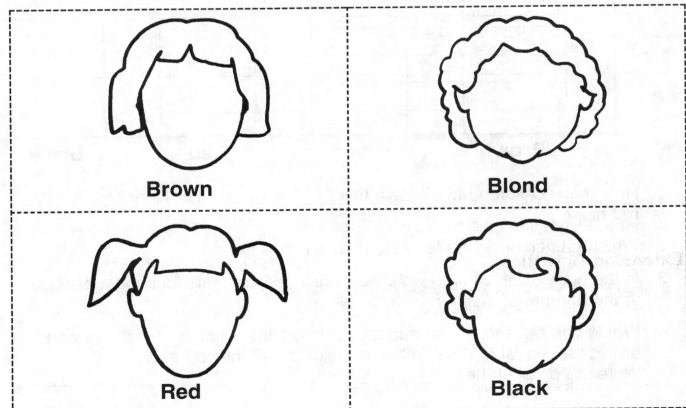

Brown

Blond

Red

Black

Hair Color *(cont.)*

OUR HAIR COLORS

Number of Students

Brown	Blond	Red	Black

1. How many children have brown hair? _____ blond hair? _____
   red hair? _____ black hair? _____

2. Which hair color do the fewest number of children have? _____

3. Is the number of children with brown hair greater than, less than, or equal
   to the number of children with blond hair?_____

4. Would you have to add or subtract to make the number of children with
   brown hair equal to the number of children with blond hair? _____
   Write the problem here: _____

Taste

Preparation:

1. Reproduce the table (page 6) and make an overhead transparency of it.
2. Reproduce the bar graph (page 59) and the response cards (page 58) for students. Make one set of response cards (Sweet, Sour, Salty) for each student.
3. Purchase a variety of foods that are sweet, sour, and salty. Some suggestions are listed below.

   Note: Be sure to ask parents if their children have any food allergies or dietary restrictions.

Sweet	Sour	Salty
candy (not sour)	sour candy	salted pretzels
dried fruit	lemon	salted peanuts
ice cream	sour cream	salted sunflower seeds
cookies	pickles	salted popcorn
sugar cubes	plain yogurt	salted potato chips

Directions:

1. Discuss how foods can have different tastes.
2. On the chalkboard, make a three-column chart with the words *Sweet, Sour,* and *Salty* as headings. Tell students that they are going to taste some foods and decide in which category these foods belong. Allow students to sample one food at a time and decide whether each tastes sweet, sour, or salty. After they decide in which category each food belongs, list it under the appropriate heading on the chart.
3. After all of the foods have been tasted, invite students to help you count how many are listed in each category on the chart. Record this data on the transparency of the table, as shown in the example below, and/or have students record it on their copies of the table.

TASTES	
Type of Taste	**Number of Foods**
Sweet	12
Sour	3
Salty	5

4. Use the floor or wall graph to model the activity. Show students how to mark the scale along the bottom, counting by ones or twos. Help students place the bars on the graph.
5. Have students work with partners to record the results on their bar graphs.
6. Discuss the questions (page 59) and ask additional ones to check students' understanding.

Extension Activities:

1. For each student, fold a piece of construction paper to divide it into three equal sections. Tell students to write the headings *Sweet, Sour,* and *Salty,* one in each section. Have them draw themselves eating something sweet, sour, and salty in the appropriate sections.
2. Divide the class into cooperative learning groups. Have students work together to create wall pictographs, using the response cards (page 58).

Taste *(cont.)*

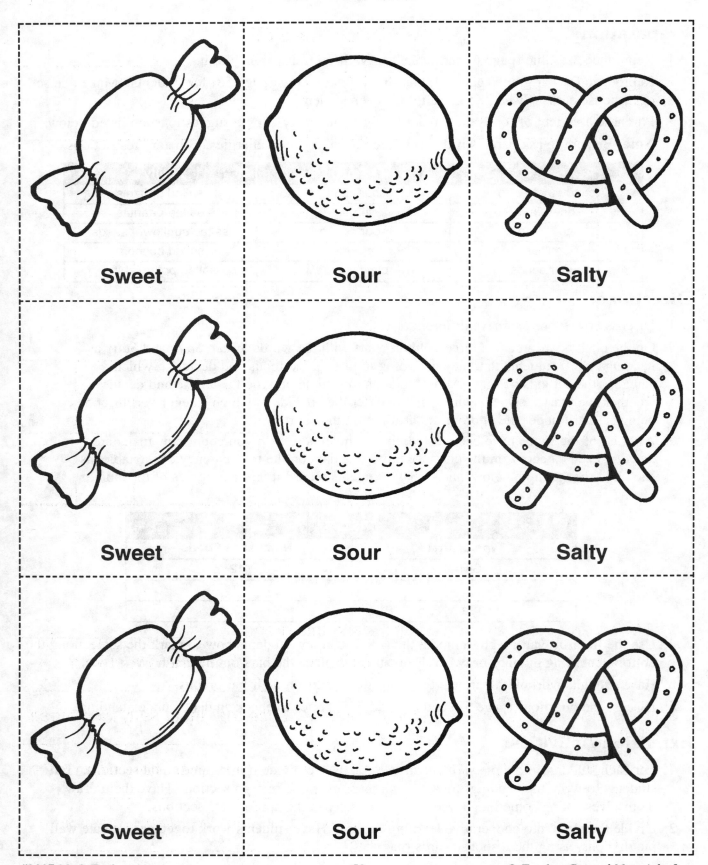

Sweet   **Sour**   **Salty**

Sweet   **Sour**   **Salty**

Sweet   **Sour**   **Salty**

58

Taste *(cont.)*

HOW FOODS TASTE

Sweet

Sour

Salty

Number of Foods

1. How many foods were tasted to make this graph? _____

2. How many foods are there if you combine those that taste sweet with those that taste sour? _____

3. How many foods are there if you combine those that taste salty with those that taste sour? _____

4. Is the number of foods that taste sweet greater than, less than, or equal to the number of foods that taste sour? _____

5. Is the number of foods that taste salty greater than, less than, or equal to the number of foods that taste sweet? _____

Muffins

Preparation:

1. Obtain a copy of the book *If You Give a Moose a Muffin* by Laura Numeroff Joffe (HarperCollins, 1991).
2. Reproduce the table (page 6) and make an overhead transparency of it.
3. Reproduce the bar graph (page 62) for students.
4. Bake or purchase blueberry, banana nut, and corn muffins. Be sure to ask parents if their children have any food allergies or dietary restrictions.

Directions:

1. Begin this activity by reading *If You Give a Moose a Muffin*. Invite volunteers to tell what kinds of muffins they have eaten in the past.
2. Cut a few of the blueberry, banana nut, and corn muffins into small pieces, making sure to keep the different types separated. Allow students to taste each type of muffin and determine which they like best. Ask each student to select her/his favorite type of muffin for snack. On the chalkboard, keep a tally of how many students choose each type of muffin. Record the total number of students who picked each type of muffin on the transparency of the table, as shown in the example below. Allow students to eat their muffins as they write the data on their copies of the table.

OUR FAVORITE MUFFINS	
Type of Muffins	**Number of Students**
Blueberry	17
Banana Nut	3
Corn	5

3. Use the floor or wall graph to model the activity. Show students how to mark the scale along the bottom, counting by ones, twos, or threes. Help students place the bars on the graph.
4. Have students record the results on their bar graphs.
5. Discuss the questions (page 62) and ask additional ones to check students' understanding.

Extension Activities:

1. Make bar graphs that include other types of muffins.
2. Create a wall or floor pictographs, using the muffin patterns (page 61).
3. Have students follow a recipe to bake the type of muffin that was the most popular.
4. If possible, provide advertisements for different types of muffin mixes. Otherwise, just create a table that shows the (real or fictional) names of mixes and their prices. Divide the class into cooperative learning groups. Ask students to do a cost comparison of the muffin mixes to determine which is the best buy.
5. Have pairs of students use rulers to measure the heights of two different muffins and scales to measure the weights. Ask them to determine which muffin is taller and which one is heavier.

Muffins *(cont.)*

Blueberry

Banana Nut

Corn

Muffins *(cont.)*

OUR FAVORITE MUFFINS

Blueberry

Banana Nut

Corn

Number of Votes

1. Which type of muffin is liked the most? _____

2. Which type of muffin is liked the least? _____

3. How many children like blueberry muffins the most? _____
    banana nut muffins? _____ corn muffins?_____

4. Were any types of muffins chosen by the same number of children?_____
    If yes, which ones? _____

5. If there were twice as many votes for each type of muffin, how many votes
    would there be for blueberry muffins? _____
    banana nut muffins? _____ corn muffins?_____

Cookies

Preparation:

1. Obtain a copy of the book *If You Give a Mouse a Cookie* by Laura Numeroff Joffe (HarperCollins, 1985).
2. Make an overhead transparency of the table (page 6).
3. Bake or purchase chocolate chip, sugar, and peanut butter cookies. Be sure to ask parents if their children have any food allergies or dietary restrictions.
4. Reproduce the bar graph (page 65) for students.

Directions:

1. Begin this activity by reading *If You Give a Mouse a Cookie*. Have students brainstorm a list of the types of cookies the mouse might have eaten.
2. Show students three types of cookies: chocolate chip, sugar, and peanut butter. Ask them to choose their favorite type of cookie for snack. Record students' choices on the transparency of the table, as shown in the example below. Allow students to eat their cookies.

OUR FAVORITE COOKIES	
Type of Cookies	**Number of Votes**
Chocolate Chip	12
Sugar	4
Peanut Butter	8

3. Use the floor or wall graph to model the activity. Show students how to mark the scale on the left-hand side, counting by ones, twos, or threes. Help students place the bars on the graph.
4. Divide the class into small groups or assign partners. Have students record the results on their bar graphs.
5. Discuss the questions (page 65) and ask additional ones to check students' understanding. Have students practice basic addition and subtraction facts by asking: *How many votes would you have to add to the _____ cookies (second most liked) to make the number equal to the _____ cookies (most liked)? How many votes would you have to take away from the _____ cookies (most liked) to make the number equal to the _____ cookies (least liked)?*

Extension Activities:

1. Create pictographs, using the cookie patterns (page 64).
2. Have students bake the type of cookie that was the most popular.
3. Provide each student with three cookies: one chocolate chip, one sugar, and one peanut butter. Have students use a balance scale to determine which type of cookie is the heaviest and which is the lightest. If you plan to have students eat the cookies when they are finished with the activity, place paper towels on the scales before putting the cookies on them.

Cookies *(cont.)*

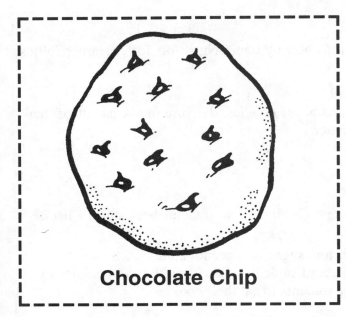

Chocolate Chip

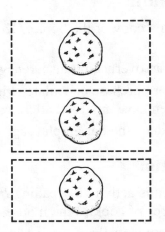

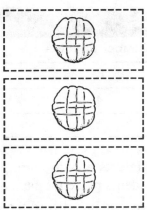

Peanut Butter

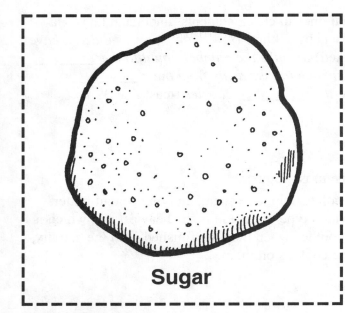

Sugar

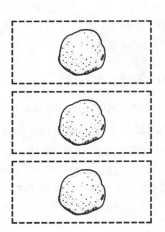

Cookies *(cont.)*

OUR FAVORITE COOKIES

Number of Votes

Chocolate Chip   **Sugar**   **Peanut Butter**

1. Which type of cookie is liked the most? _____

2. Which type of cookie is liked the least? _____

3. How many children like peanut butter cookies the most? _____
   sugar cookies? _____ chocolate chip cookies? _____

4. Were any types of cookies chosen by the same number of children? _____
   If yes, which ones? _____

Pets

Preparation:

1. Obtain a copy of the book *The Puppy Who Wanted a Boy* by Jane Thayer (William Morrow, 1958).
2. Reproduce the table (page 6) and make an overhead transparency of it.
3. Reproduce the large pet patterns (page 67) and the bar graph (page 68) for students. Cut apart the patterns.

Directions:

1. Begin this activity by reading *The Puppy Who Wanted a Boy*. Use the story to initiate a discussion about what a pet is. Ask students to brainstorm a list of animals that make good pets.
2. Show students the four pet patterns: Dog, Cat, Dog and Cat, No Dog or Cat. Explain that students who have one or more dogs without any cats should take the *Dog* patterns. Those with one or more cats without any dogs should take the *Cat* patterns. Students with one or more cats in addition to one or more dogs should take the *Dog and Cat* patterns. However, students who do not have a cat or a dog should take the *No Dog or Cat* patterns. Allow a few students at a time to take the patterns that show what kind of pet(s) they have at home.
3. As you call each pet listed on the table, have students raise their patterns if they have that kind of pet. Invite the class to help you count the patterns to determine how many students have each type of pet. Record the data on the transparency of the table, as shown in the example below. Have students write the data on their copies of the table.

OUR PETS	
Type of Pet	**Number of Students**
Dog	12
Cat	8
Dog and Cat	4
No Dog or Cat	5

4. Use the floor or wall graph to model the activity. Show students how to mark the scale along the bottom, counting by ones, twos, or threes. Help students place the bars on the graph.
5. Divide the class into small groups or assign partners. Have students record the results on their bar graphs.
6. Discuss the questions (page 68) and ask additional ones to check students' understanding.

Extension Activities:

1. Create pictographs, using the small pet patterns (page 67).
2. Invite a veterinarian to speak to your class about pet care.
3. Using the list of pets students have generated in Step 1 of the Directions, have them classify the animals into groups: mammals, birds, fish, reptiles, and amphibians.
4. Ask students to bring their favorite stuffed animals. Sort these toys into groups by what kind of animals they are. Have students create bar graphs to show this information.

Pets (cont.)

Dog

Cat

Dog and Cat

No Dog or Cat

Pets *(cont.)*

OUR PETS

Dog

Cat

Dog and Cat

No Dog or Cat

Number of Students

1. Which type of pet do most of the children have? _____

2. Which type of pet do the fewest number of children have?_____

3. How many children have dogs? _____ cats? _____
   dogs and cats? _____ no dog or cat? _____

4. Would you have to add or subtract to make the number of children who own cats equal to the number of children who own dogs? _____ How many would you have to add or subtract?_____

5. Is the number of children who own dogs added to the number of children who own cats greater than, less than, or equal to the number of children who own both dogs and cats? _____

Pizza

Preparation:

1. Reproduce the table (page 6) and make an overhead transparency of it.
2. Reproduce the large pizza patterns (page 70) and the bar graph (page 71) for students.
3. Make or purchase cheese, pepperoni, hamburger, and vegetarian pizza. There should be enough for students to have a taste of each type. Be sure to ask parents if their children have any food allergies or dietary restrictions.

Directions:

1. Provide the four types of pizza and allow students to have a small piece of each.
2. While students are tasting the pizzas, distribute the large pizza patterns. Be sure to give all four patterns to each student. After students have tasted the pizzas, ask them to arrange the patterns in order from most liked to least liked.
3. Make a four-column chart on the chalkboard with the headings *Cheese, Pepperoni, Hamburger,* and *Vegetarian*. Ask each student to tell which is his/her favorite type of pizza and place a tally mark on the chalkboard under the appropriate heading. After everyone has written a tally mark, invite students to help you count the total number of votes for each type of pizza. (**Note:** As an alternative, you can have students raise the pattern of their favorite pizzas when you call out the names listed on the table. Then students can help you count the number of patterns raised for each type of pizza.) Record the total number of votes for each type of pizza on the transparency of the table, as shown in the example below. If possible, give each student a whole slice of his/her favorite type of pizza. Have students write the data on their copies of the table.

OUR FAVORITE PIZZAS	
Type of Pizza	**Number of Votes**
Cheese	10
Pepperoni	6
Hamburger	4
Vegetarian	4

4. Use the floor or wall graph to model the activity. Show students how to mark the scale on the left-hand side, counting by ones, twos, or threes. Help students place the bars on the graph.
5. Have students record the results on their bar graphs.
6. Discuss the questions (page 71) and ask additional ones to check students' understanding. Have students practice basic addition and subtraction facts by asking: *How many votes would you have to add to the* _____ *pizza (second most liked) to make the number equal to the* _____ *pizza (most liked)? How many votes would you have to take away from the* _____ *pizza (most liked) to make the number equal to the* _____ *pizza (least liked)?*

Extension Activities:

1. Create pictographs, using the small pizza patterns (page 70).
2. Have students make the type of pizza that is the most popular.

Pizza *(cont.)*

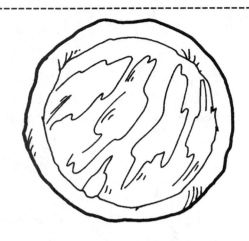

Cheese

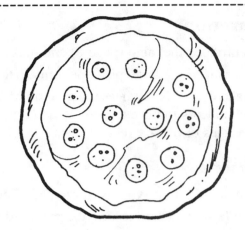

Pepperoni

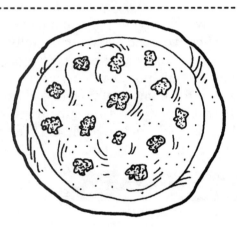

Hamburger

Vegetarian

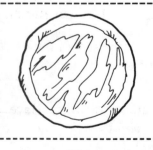
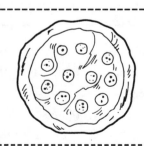

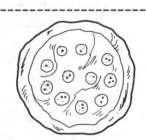

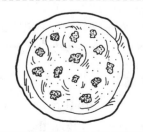

Pizza *(cont.)*

OUR FAVORITE PIZZAS

Number of Votes

Cheese	Pepperoni	Hamburger	Vegetarian

1. Which type of pizza is liked the most? _____

2. Which type of pizza is liked the least? _____

3. How many children like cheese pizza the most? _____
   pepperoni? _____   hamburger? _____   vegetarian? _____

4. Were any types of pizza chosen by the same number of children? _____
   If yes, which ones? _____

5. Is the number of votes for pepperoni pizza greater than, less than, or equal
   to the number of votes for hamburger pizza? _____

Colors

Preparation:

1. Reproduce the table (page 6) and make an overhead transparency of it.
2. Reproduce the bar graph (page 73) for students.
3. Provide pieces of construction paper, one of each color: red, blue, green, yellow, orange, purple.

Directions:

1. Begin this activity by having students brainstorm a list of colors. Write the color words on the chalkboard.
2. Show students the red, blue, green, yellow, orange, and purple pieces of construction paper. Tell them that you are going to pass around these pieces of paper. Explain that each student should write his/her name on the piece of paper that is his/her favorite color. Point out that each student should write his/her name only once.
3. Make sure every student has written his/her name on one of the pieces of construction paper. Then ask volunteers to count the total number of names written on each piece of paper. Record the results on the transparency of the table, as shown in the example below. Ask students to write the data on their copies of the table.

OUR FAVORITE COLORS	
Colors	**Number of Votes**
Red	4
Blue	6
Green	5
Yellow	1
Orange	4
Purple	5

4. Use the floor or wall graph to model the activity. Show students how to mark the scale along the bottom, counting by ones, twos, or threes. Help students place the bars on the graph.
5. Have students record the results on their bar graphs.
6. Discuss the questions (page 73) and ask additional ones to check students' understanding. Have students practice basic addition and subtraction facts by asking: *How many votes would you have to add to _____ (second most liked color) to make the number equal to _____ (most liked color)? How many votes would you have to take away from _____ (most liked color) to make the number equal to _____ (least liked color)?*

Extension Activities:

1. Create pictographs, using construction paper squares that match students' favorite colors.
2. Have students learn about the colors of the rainbow. Teach them the order of the colors, using the name ROY G. BIV (red, orange, yellow, green, blue, indigo, violet).
3. Encourage students to make a list of objects in the classroom that are their favorite colors. You may wish to have students who share the same favorite color work together in small groups.

Colors *(cont.)*

OUR FAVORITE COLORS

Red	MWM	GM	TB	TC					
Blue	MWM	GM	TB	TC	RP	MW			
Green	ALP	TC	RP	MW					
Yellow	MWM	ALP							
Orange	TB	RP	TB MW						
Purple	TB	ALP	TB						

Number of Votes

1. Which color is liked the most? _____

2. Which color is liked the least? _____

3. Is the number of votes for yellow and purple together greater than, less than, or equal to the number of votes for orange and green together?

   _____

4. Is the number of votes for blue and red together greater than, less than, or equal to the number of votes for blue and purple together? _____

5. If twice as many children voted for each color, how many votes would there be for red? _____ blue? _____ green? _____ yellow? _____ orange? _____ purple? _____

Temperature

Preparation:

1. Make an overhead transparency of the large thermometer (page 75).
2. Reproduce the small thermometers (page 75) and line graph (page 76) for students.
3. Provide thermometers for students to use. If you only have one thermometer, be sure all students have the opportunity to observe the temperature on it.
4. **Optional:** Reproduce the table (page 6) and make an overhead transparency of it.

Directions:

1. Show students how to read a thermometer, using the transparency of the large thermometer. Point out the difference between the Fahrenheit and Celsius scales. If you prefer to present only one of the scales, cut the transparency in half up the middle of the thermometer.
2. Early in the morning, have students place their thermometers outside in a safe place.
3. At regular intervals throughout the day, have students read the thermometers six times and record the data by using red crayons to color the small thermometers. You may need to help students read and record the time before checking the thermometers.
4. **Optional:** Have students record the data from their colored thermometers on tables. Demonstrate how to do this, using the transparency of the table, as shown in the example below.

TEMPERATURES ON _____ (Date)	
Time	**Temperature**
9:00 A.M.	68° F (20° C)
10:00 A.M.	70° F (21° C)
11:00 A.M.	72° F (22° C)
12:00 P.M.	75° F (24° C)
1:00 P.M.	80° F (26° C)
2:00 P.M.	83° F (28° C)

5. Model how to mark the scales and record the temperatures on the floor or wall graph.
6. Assign or allow students to pick partners. Have students record the data on their line graphs.
7. Discuss the questions (page 76) and ask additional ones to check students' understanding.

Extension Activities:

1. Measure the temperature at the same time each day for a period of time such as a week.
2. Discuss the difference between warm-blooded and cold-blooded animals.
3. Discuss how temperature affects people. Topics include clothing, shelter, and agriculture.
4. Use the local newspaper to collect data about the daily high and low temperatures in your community over one week. Then have each student create a line graph, using a red line to connect the highs and a blue line to connect the lows.

Temperature *(cont.)*

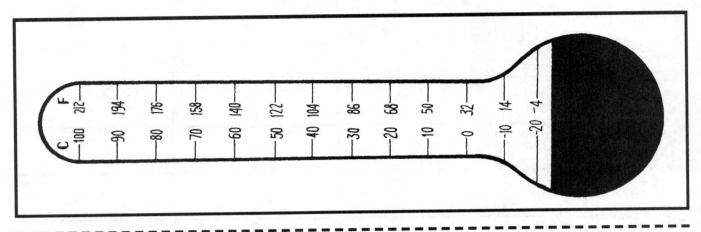

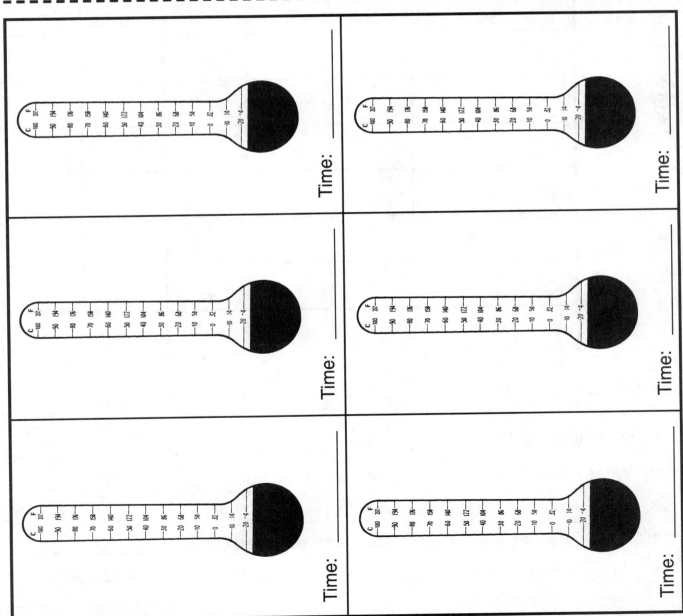

Time: _____

Time: _____

Time: _____

Time: _____

Time: _____

Time: _____

#2007 Math Explorations

Temperature *(cont.)*

TEMPERATURES ON _____

(Date)

Degrees (°)

Time

1. What was the highest temperature? _____

2. What time was the highest temperature recorded?_____

3. What was the lowest temperature? _____

4. What time was the lowest temperature recorded? _____

5. What is the difference between the highest and lowest temperatures?

_____

Precipitation

Preparation:

1. Obtain or make a rain gauge. As an alternative, students can use a local newspaper or weather reports on the radio or television to obtain data about the amount of precipitation in your community.
2. Reproduce the line graph (page 78) for students.
3. Reproduce the table (page 6) and make an overhead transparency of it.

Directions:

1. Show students how to read a rain gauge, using inches and/or centimeters.
2. Place the rain gauge outside in a safe place.
3. Decide how frequently (daily, weekly, or monthly) you want students to check the gauge, as well as how many times you want them to collect data. On the transparency of the table, complete the left-hand column accordingly.
4. Assign or allow students to pick partners. Have the partners read the rain gauge at the same time each day they collect data. (**Note:** Students' measurements may vary slightly.) Have them record the data on their copies of the table. You may wish to demonstrate how to do this, using the transparency of the table, as shown in the example below.

PRECIPITATION	
Date	**Precipitation**
Oct. 1	0.1 in. (0.3 cm)
Oct. 2	0.25 in. (0.6 cm)
Oct. 3	0.25 in. (0.6 cm)
Oct. 4	1.0 in. (2.5 cm)
Oct. 5	1.0 in. (2.5 cm)

5. Model how to mark the scales and record the temperatures on a floor or wall line graph.
6. Have students record the data on their line graphs.
7. Discuss the questions (page 78) and ask additional ones to check students' understanding.

Extension Activities:

1. Have students draw diagrams of the water cycle.
2. Invite students to write poems about different types of precipitation, such as snow, sleet, hail, and rain. Mount the poems on snowflake or raindrop cutouts. Display the poetry on a bulletin board in the classroom or the library.
3. Discuss the problems of water pollution. Have students brainstorm a list of ways that people can help reduce the amount of water pollution.
4. Divide the class into cooperative learning groups. Ask students to work together to tell what is good and bad about a rainy day. Allow time for each group to share their information.
5. Read aloud *A Snow Day* by Ezra Jack Keats (Viking, 1976). Encourage students to draw pictures of themselves on a snowy day.

Precipitation (cont.)

OUR PRECIPITATION

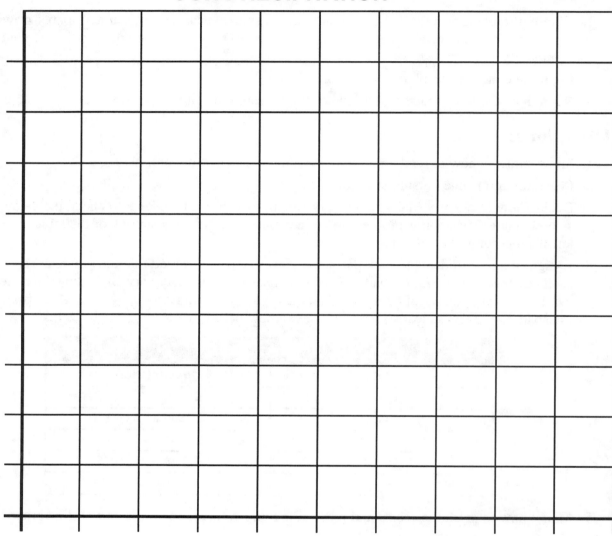

Inches (Cm)

Dates

1. On which date or dates did the greatest amount of precipitation fall?

   _____

2. What was the largest amount of precipitation measured?_____

3. On which date or dates did the amount of precipitation **increase** over the time before? _____

4. On which date or dates did the amount of precipitation **decrease** over the time before? _____

5. What was the total amount of precipitation? _____

78

Plant Growth

Preparation:

1. Provide seeds, Styrofoam cups, and soil.
2. Reproduce the line graph (page 80) for students.
3. Provide rulers if students do not already have some. Make a transparency of the ruler shown at the bottom of this page.
4. Reproduce the table (page 6) and make an overhead transparency of it.

Directions:

1. Use the ruler transparency to show how to measure in inches and/or centimeters.
2. Assign partners. Have the pairs of students plant a few seeds in Styrofoam cups according to the directions on the package. After the plants start to grow, ask each pair to select and mark one plant to measure. Other seeds that germinate can be replanted in a separate cup, if desired.
3. On the transparency of the table, list the dates on which measurements should be taken.
4. Have students record the data on their copies of the table. You may wish to demonstrate how to do this using the transparency of the table, as shown in the example below.

PLANT GROWTH	
Date	**Amount of Growth**
Sept. 7	0.5 in. (1.3 cm)
Sept. 10	0.25 in. (0.6 cm)
Sept. 13	1.0 in. (2.5 cm)
Sept. 16	1.3 in. (3.3 cm)
Sept. 19	0.8 in. (2.0 cm)
Sept. 22	0.5 in. (1.3 cm)

5. Model how to mark the scales and record the plant growth on a floor or wall line graph.
6. Have students record the data on their line graphs.
7. Discuss the questions (page 80) and ask additional ones to check students' understanding.

Extension Activities:

Obtain permission for students to plant a garden on the school grounds. Allow them to plan the organization of the garden. Then show them how to plant, care for, and harvest the different kinds of plants.

Ruler

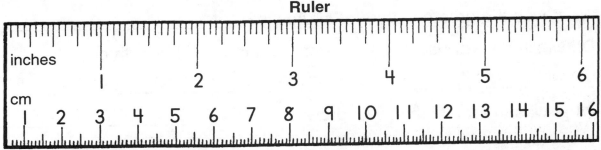

Plant Growth (cont.)

HOW MUCH OUR PLANT GREW

Inches (Cm)

Dates

1. On which date or dates did the greatest amount of growth occur?_____

   _____

2. What was the greatest amount of growth? _____

3. On which date or dates did the smallest amount of growth occur?_____

   _____

4. What was the total amount of growth? _____

Height

Preparation:

1. Obtain a tape measure or a scale that can be used to measure students' heights.
2. Reproduce the line graph (page 82) for students.
3. Draw a table on the chalkboard. Write students' names in the left-hand column.

Directions:

1. Throughout the school year, on the same day of the month for six consecutive months, use the scale or tape measure to determine the height of each student. You may wish to solicit the help of a parent volunteer or older student for this. Each time, record the data in a table drawn on the chalkboard as shown in the example below.

HEIGHT	
Name of Student	**Height**
Tom	36 in. (91 cm)
Andrea	41 in. (104 cm)
Felicia	44 in. (112 cm)
José	39 in. (99 cm)
Daniel	35 in. (89 cm)
Susan	40 in. (102 cm)

2. The first time a measurement is taken, model how to mark the scales and record a height on the floor or wall line graph. Each time thereafter, model how to record the new height and draw lines to connect the measurements.
3. Each time students are measured, have them record their heights on the line graphs.
4. Discuss the questions (page 82) and ask additional ones to check students' understanding.

Extension Activities:

1. Mount a tape measure on a door or wall, making sure the zero mark is flush with the floor. Each time students are measured, use yarn and slips of paper with students' names to mark their heights on the tape measure. Each time students are remeasured, attach new pieces of yarn and slips of paper with students' names. Leave this up throughout the year.
2. Invite students to make bar graphs to compare their heights to the heights of four friends.
3. Have each student make a line graph that shows her/his height and the height of another person, such as a friend or family member, over a period of months. Ask students to compare/contrast their rate of growth with those of the other people shown on their graphs.
4. Provide students with additional practice using rulers for measurement. Ask them to measure the heights of different objects in the classroom.
5. Encourage students to use their imaginations and write stories describing what life would be like being the tallest or smallest person in the world.

Height *(cont.)*

My Height

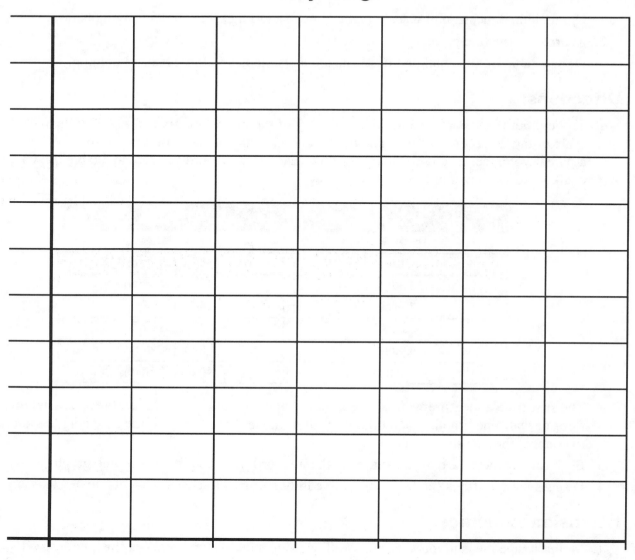

Inches (Cm)

Measurement Dates

1. On which date did you have the greatest increase in height?_____

2. On which date did you have the smallest increase in height?_____

3. Were there any measurement dates on which you did not show any growth? _____ If yes, which dates? _____

4. Over the time of the first three measurements, did you grow more or less than over the time of the last three measurements? _____

5. What was your total amount of growth? _____

Weight

Preparation:

1. Obtain a scale that can be used to measure students' weights.
2. Reproduce the line graph (page 84) for students.
3. Draw a table on the chalkboard. Write students' names in the left-hand column.

Directions:

Note: This issue of weight may be a sensitive one for some children. Keep this in mind as you use this activity and adjust as necessary.

1. Throughout the school year, on the same day for six consecutive months, use the scale to determine the weight of each student. You may wish to solicit the help of a parent volunteer or older student for this. Each time, record the data in a table drawn on the chalkboard as shown in the example below.

WEIGHT	
Name of Student	**Weight**
Tina	50 lbs. (23 kg)
Greg	52 lbs. (24 kg)
Phillip	67 lbs. (31 kg)
Alexis	60 lbs. (27 kg)
Jermaine	61 lbs. (28 kg)
Wendy	48 lbs. (22 kg)

2. The first time a measurement is taken, model how to mark the scales and record a weight on the floor or wall line graph. Each time thereafter, model how to record the new weight and draw lines to connect the measurements.
3. Each time students are weighed, have them record their weights on the line graphs.
4. Discuss the questions (page 84) and ask additional ones to check students' understanding.

Extension Activities:

1. Ask students to bring a variety of empty food packages or provide these yourself. Have them identify the weights on the different packages. Give each student three packages. Tell students to place their packages in order from lightest to heaviest.
2. Invite students to make bar graphs to compare their weights to the weights of four friends.
3. Have each student make a line graph that shows her/his weight and the weight of another person, such as a friend or family member, over a period of months. Ask students to compare/contrast their weights with those of the other people shown on their graphs.
4. Allow students to practice using scales for measuring weight. Ask them to measure the weights of different objects in the classroom.
5. Encourage students to use their imaginations and write stories describing what life would be like on a planet with no gravity, giving them the feeling of being weightless.

Weight *(cont.)*

My Weight

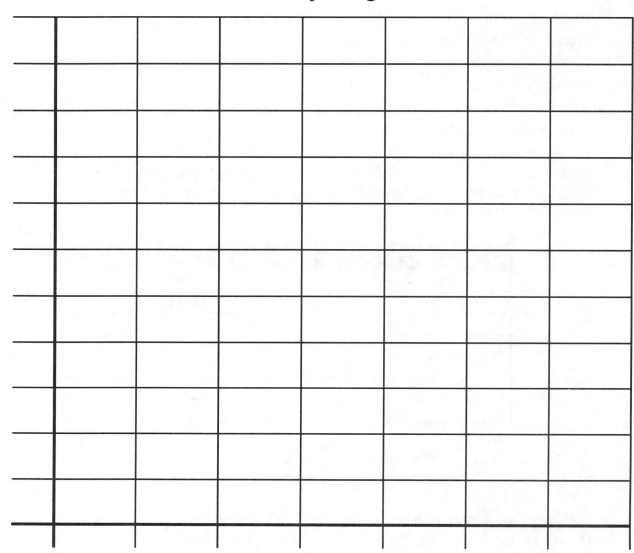

Pounds (Kg)

Dates

1. On which date did you have the greatest increase in weight? _____

2. On which date did you have the smallest increase in weight? _____

3. Were there any dates on which you showed a decrease in weight? _____
   If yes, which dates? _____

4. Over the time of the first three measurements, did you gain more or less
   weight than over the time of the last three measurements? _____

5. What was your total amount of weight gain?_____

Coins

Preparation:

1. Reproduce the table (page 6) for students and make an overhead transparency of it.
2. Reproduce the line graph (page 86).
3. Provide one set of coins (plastic or real) for each pair or group of students. The number of each type of coin (pennies, nickels, dimes, quarters, half dollars) can vary. Place the coins in reclosable plastic bags or envelopes, making all of the sets exactly the same. (**Note:** For younger students, limit the types of coins to one or two, such as pennies or pennies and nickels.) Change the sets of coins every day for one week. With each change, the number of each type of coin can increase, decrease, or remain the same as the time before. Remember to make all of the sets exactly the same and to place the coins back in the plastic bags or envelopes.

Directions:

1. Divide the class into small groups or assign partners. Have students count the coins in the bags and record the data on their tables. You may wish to demonstrate how to do this, using the transparency of the table, as shown in the example below.

Number of Coins—Day 1	
Type of Coin	**Number of Coins**
Penny	5
Nickel	3
Dime	3
Quarter	2
Half Dollar	1

2. Model how to mark the scales and record the data on the floor or wall line graph.
3. Then have students mark their line graphs according to the data. Tell them to use different colors for the different types of coins.
4. The next day change the sets of coins and have students repeat the procedure of collecting and recording the data. Continue in this manner for one week. Check students' work to ensure accuracy. If necessary, help them draw the lines to connect the colored dots they make.
5. At the end of the week, discuss the questions (page 86) and ask additional ones to check students' understanding.

Extension Activities:

1. Teach students about probability using the coins. After determining the number of each coin, have students replace them in the bags or envelopes. Then have students make predictions about which coins are most likely, least likely, or equally likely to be drawn. (*The coin with the greatest number will most likely be drawn. The one with the fewest will least likely be drawn. Coins that have the same number will have an equal chance of being drawn.*)
2. Have students create stacks of coins. Ask them to determine how many pennies, nickels, dimes, quarters, and half dollars would be needed for each stack to measure 1 inch (2.5 cm).

Coins (cont.)

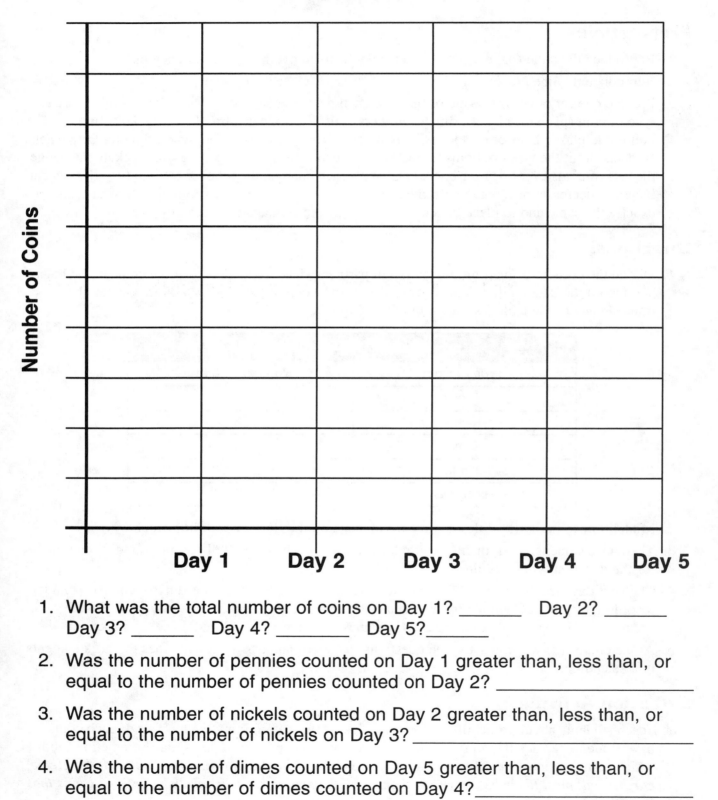

Number of Coins

Day 1   Day 2   Day 3   Day 4   Day 5

1. What was the total number of coins on Day 1? _____ Day 2? _____ Day 3? _____ Day 4? _____ Day 5?_____

2. Was the number of pennies counted on Day 1 greater than, less than, or equal to the number of pennies counted on Day 2? _____

3. Was the number of nickels counted on Day 2 greater than, less than, or equal to the number of nickels on Day 3? _____

4. Was the number of dimes counted on Day 5 greater than, less than, or equal to the number of dimes counted on Day 4?_____

5. Was the number of quarters counted on Day 4 greater than, less than, or equal to the number of halfdollars counted on Day 4? _____

Books

Preparation:

1. Reproduce the line graph (page 88) for students.
2. Reproduce the table (page 6) and make an overhead transparency of it.

Directions:

1. Tell students that they are going to keep track of how many pages they read each day for a week. For this activity, you can use books that they are reading independently, books that they are reading together as a class, or a book that you are reading aloud to the class.
2. Each day allocate some time for students to do the reading. As an alternative, you can assign the reading for homework.
3. Have students record the number of pages they read on their copies of the table. Demonstrate how to do this using the transparency of the table, as shown in the example below.

BOOKS	
Date	**Number of Pages Read**
Jan. 7	3
Jan. 8	4
Jan. 9	6
Jan. 10	3
Jan. 11	5
Jan. 12	7

4. Model how to mark the scales and record the data on the floor or wall line graph.
5. Have students record the data on their line graphs.
6. Discuss the questions (page 88) and ask additional ones to check students' understanding.

Extension Activities:

1. Have students create line graphs that show how many books they read each month. Ask them to compare and contrast the different months.
2. Encourage students to make book covers for their favorite books. Tell them to be sure to show the title and author's name on each cover.
3. Take students to the public library. Ask them to compare it with the school library.
4. Reproduce the small book patterns shown at the bottom of this page. Invite students to use the patterns to create pictographs.

Books *(cont.)*

Number of Pages Read

Dates

1. On which date or dates did you read more pages than the time before?

    _____

2. On which date or dates did you read fewer pages than the time before?

    _____

3. What was the greatest number of pages that you read in one day?_____

4. What was the fewest number of pages that you read in one day? _____

5. What was the total number of pages you read? _____

Endangered Species

Preparation:

1. Reproduce the game board (pages 90–93) and set of playing cards (pages 94 and 95), one for every two or three students.

2. Glue the playing cards onto construction paper. Allow the glue to dry. Then laminate, cut out, and place each set of playing cards in a reclosable plastic bag.

3. Construct each game board as follows: Cut off the top and right side of page 90. Cut off the bottom of page 91. Align and tape page 91 above page 90. Align and tape page 92 to the right of page 90. Cut off the bottom of page 93. Align and tape page 93 to the right of page 91 and above page 92. Rewrite the number 5 on both the vertical and horizontal axes. Glue the game boards onto poster board or tagboard. You may wish to laminate the game boards.

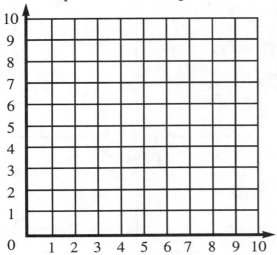

Answer Key

Giant Panda (7, 6)	Black Rhinoceros (3, 9)
Polar Bear (9, 7)	Kemp's Ridley Turtle (7, 1)
Key Deer (6, 7)	Aye-Aye (8, 8)
Cheetah (3, 6)	Whooping Crane (1, 3)
Mountain Lion (8, 4)	Manatee (4, 8)
Harp Seal (9, 3)	Prairie Dog (2, 7)
Bald Eagle (9, 2)	Humpback Whale (9, 9)
Timber Wolf (7, 2)	Koala (1, 1)
Mountain Gorilla (6, 9)	Horned Lizard (3, 8)
African Elephant (6, 3)	Sea Otter (1, 8)
American Alligator (4, 1)	Tiger (2, 2)
Gray Kangaroo (4, 3)	Mountain Goat (3, 4)

Directions:

1. Provide a game board and set of playing cards for every two or three students.

2. Model how to play the game by drawing a playing card, matching the endangered animal shown on the card with its picture on the graph, and writing its coordinates. Be sure students understand that they must move to the right for the first number and then up for the second number. If students have difficulty remembering this, use a highlighter to color the numbers at the bottom of the game board. Tell them to always start by moving along the highlighted numbers.

3. Have students record their answers on separate sheets of paper. Challenge students to see if they can get all of the answers correct. You may wish to create answer key cards for students to check themselves at the end of the game.

Extension Activities:

1. Create a real graph, using stuffed or plastic endangered animals. Have students place the animals on the graph and name the coordinates or have them place the animals on coordinates that you specify.

2. Assign an endangered animal from the playing cards (pages 94 and 95) to students. Help them research to learn where the endangered animals live and locate these places on a world map.

3. Learn about what types of endangered animals live in your area. Discuss the reasons for their endangerment. Have students brainstorm a list of things people can do to help these animals.

Endangered Species *(cont.)*

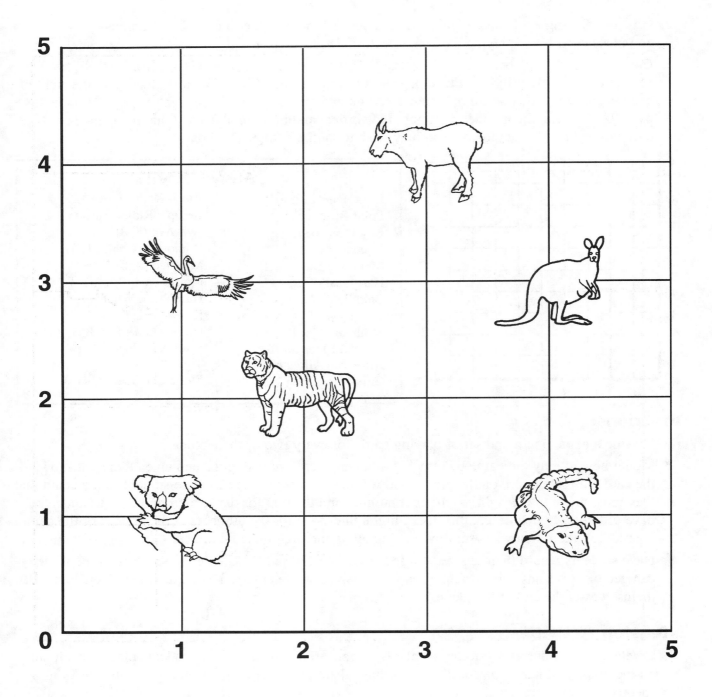

Endangered Species (cont.)

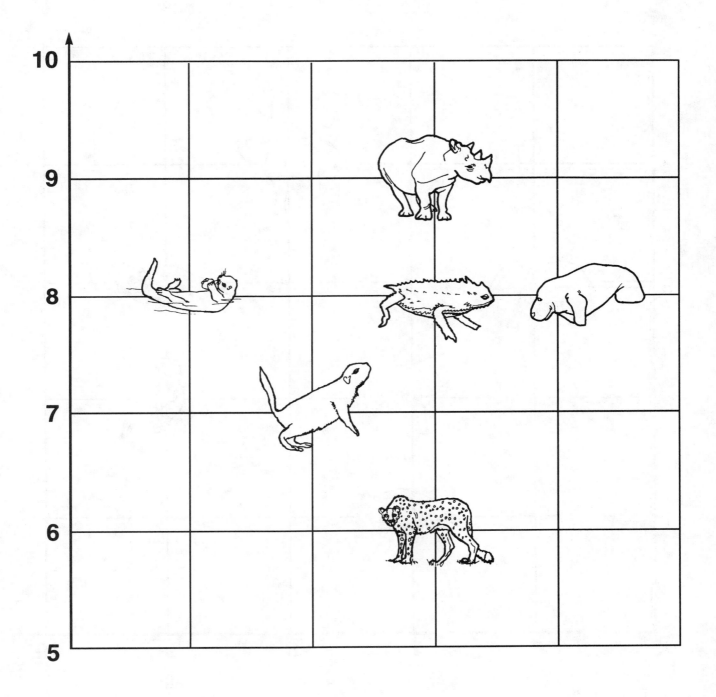

Endangered Species *(cont.)*

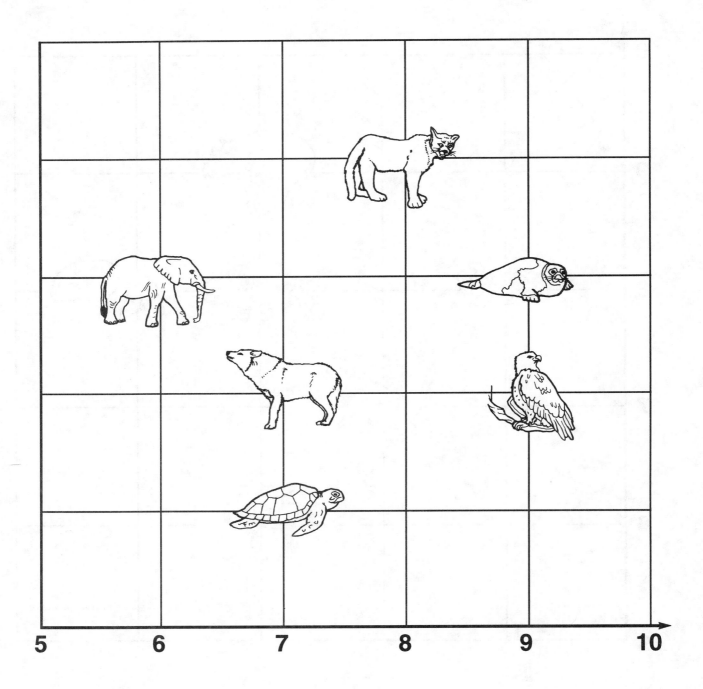

Endangered Species *(cont.)*

Endangered Species *(cont.)*

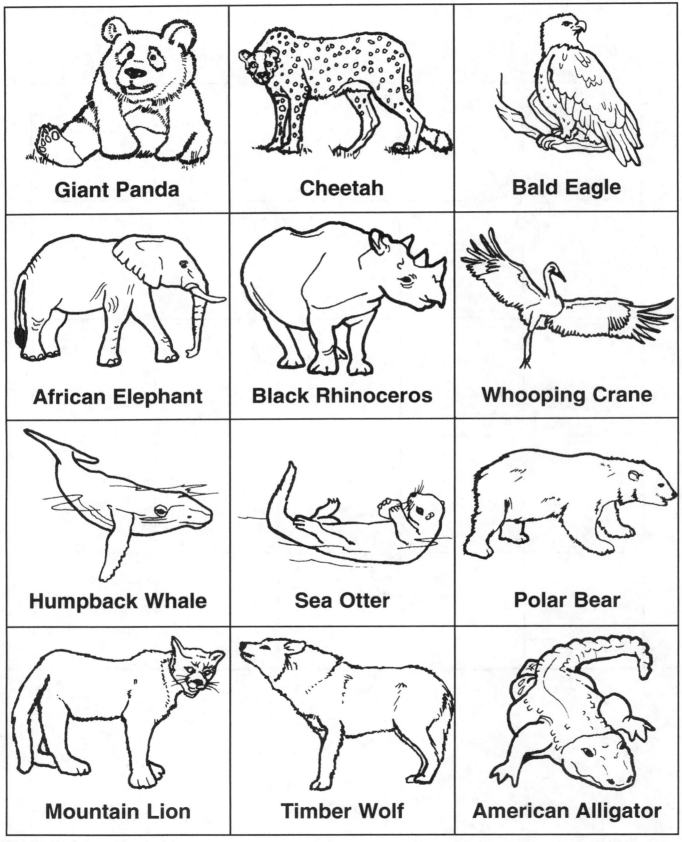

Giant Panda	Cheetah	Bald Eagle
African Elephant	Black Rhinoceros	Whooping Crane
Humpback Whale	Sea Otter	Polar Bear
Mountain Lion	Timber Wolf	American Alligator

Endangered Species (cont.)

Kemp's Ridley Turtle   Manatee   Koala

Tiger   Key Deer   Harp Seal

Mountain Gorilla   Gray Kangaroo   Aye-Aye

Prairie Dog   Horned Lizard   Mountain Goat

Treasure Hunt

Preparation:

1. Reproduce the treasure map and directions (pages 97 and 98) for students.
2. You may wish to assign partners.

Directions:

1. Distribute the treasure maps and directions to students.
2. Tell students to imagine that they are looking for a lost treasure. Explain that as they search they are drawing a map and writing the directions so they will remember how to get back to the treasure once they have found it. Point out that they must use the grid lines on the map to identify the coordinates for each landmark they see along the way.
3. As students follow the directions, have them write the coordinates to identify the locations of the specified landmarks. Be sure students understand that they must move to the right for the first number and then up for the second number. If students have difficulty remembering this, use a highlighter to color the numbers at the bottom of the graph. Tell them to always start by moving along the highlighted numbers.
4. Have students use markers or crayons to trace the route on their maps according to the directions.
5. You may wish to create answer key cards for students to check themselves at the end of the activity.

Answer Key

1. pick and shovel—(4, 0)
2. palms form an X—(4, 2)
3. sand dollar—(2, 1)
4. pail and shovel—(1, 0)
5. beach umbrella and towel—(3, 3)
6. diver's mask and fins—(3, 4)
7. sandcastle—(5, 5); quicksand—(4, 4)
8. starfish—(5, 4); anchor—(5, 3)
9. rowboat—(1, 3)
10. treasure chest—(1, 2)

Extension Activities:

1. Have students use copies of the coordinate graph (page 9) to create their own treasure maps and directions.
2. Ask students to write a story that tells about the adventures they had while searching for the lost treasure.
3. Encourage students to make treasure chests from cardboard boxes. Allow them to use a variety of objects, such as stones, marbles, beads, glitter, and confetti, to represent the treasure.
4. Read to students about famous pirates such as Jean Laffite.
5. Hide a "treasure chest" full of candy or other snacks somewhere in the classroom. Provide coordinate graphs of the classroom and directions for students. Invite students to use their graphs and directions to locate the treasure chest. After the treasure is located, allow students to enjoy the snacks.

Treasure Hunt *(cont.)*

Fill in the blanks with the correct coordinates to complete the directions for the treasure map on page 98. Remember to name the number of lines you move to the right first and then the number of lines you move up. The first one is done for you.

1. Begin by getting your pick and shovel at _____**(4, 0)**_____ .

2. Walk to the two palm trees that form an X at _____ .

3. Locate the sand dollar at _____ .

4. Continue on to the pail of sand and shovel at _____ .

5. Go above the sand dollar and over the sand dunes until you reach the beach umbrella and towel at _____ .

6. Move in a straight line until you find a diver's mask and fins at

   _____ .

7. Go to the sand castle at _____ .
   Watch out for the quicksand at _____ .

8. Walk beyond the starfish at _____ to the
   anchor at _____ .

9. From the anchor, return to the beach umbrella and cross back over the sand dunes to get the rowboat at _____ .

10. Follow the footprints in the sand from the rowboat to the treasure which is located at_____ .

       #2007 Math Explorations

Treasure Hunt (cont.)

As you complete the directions on page 97, trace the correct route to the treasure on the map shown below.

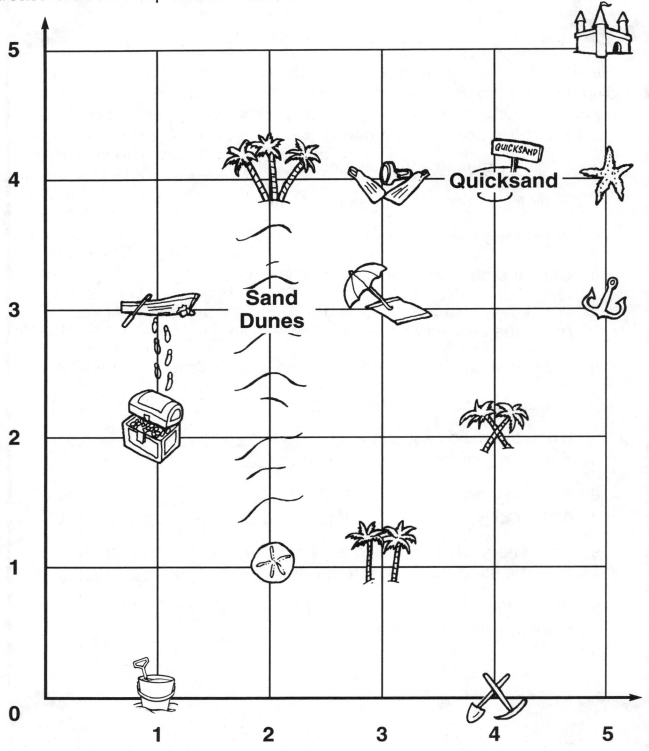

Alphabet

Preparation:

1. Reproduce the alphabet cards (pages 100–102) and the coordinate graph (page 103) for each pair of students.
2. Glue the alphabet cards onto construction paper. Allow the glue to dry. Then laminate, cut out, and place each set in a reclosable plastic bag.

Directions:

1. Tell students that they are going to play a game to practice matching uppercase and lowercase letters while using coordinate graphs. Explain that each pair of students will be given a set of alphabet cards that show uppercase letters and a coordinate graph that shows lowercase letters.
2. Model how to play the game. Begin by shuffling the alphabet cards. Place the cards face down. Demonstrate how to pick a card from the top of the stack, identify the uppercase letter on it, and match that letter with the correct lowercase letter on the coordinate graph.
3. On the chalkboard, write the coordinates for the matching lowercase letter. Be sure students understand that they must move to the right for the first number and then up for the second number. If students have difficulty remembering this, use a highlighter to color the numbers at the bottom of the coordinate graph. Tell them to always start by moving along the highlighted numbers.
4. Have each pair of students take turns drawing an alphabet card from the stack and identifying the matching letter on the graph. Ask students to use separate sheets of paper to record the coordinates for each letter. Remind them to write the letters and answers in the order that the alphabet cards are drawn rather than alphabetical order. Challenge students to see if they can get all of the answers correct. You may wish to create answer key cards for students to check themselves at the end of the game.

	Answer Key	
A, a—(9,8)	J, j—(8,3)	S, s—(6,1)
B, b—(1,9)	K, k—(2,7)	T, t—(5,10)
C, c—(7,5)	L, l—(4,10)	U, u—(0,4)
D, d—(3,6)	M, m—(9,1)	V, v—(8,9)
E, e—(7,2)	N, n—(5,4)	W, w—(3,4)
F, f—(10,5)	O, o—(8,7)	X, x—(4,2)
G, g—(1,2)	P, p—(4,6)	Y, y—(1,5)
H, h—(6,8)	Q, q—(10,3)	Z, z—(2,1)
I, i—(2,0)	R, r—(3,9)	

Extension Activities:

Rather than using the alphabet cards, you can call out letters at random and have students write the coordinates, or students can write the uppercase letters in alphabetical order and write the coordinates for the matching lowercase letters.

Alphabet *(cont.)*

A	B	C
D	E	F
G	H	I

| *100* |

Alphabet *(cont.)*

J	K	L
M	N	O
P	Q	R

Alphabet (cont.)

S	T	U
V	W	X
Y	Z	

102

Alphabet (cont.)

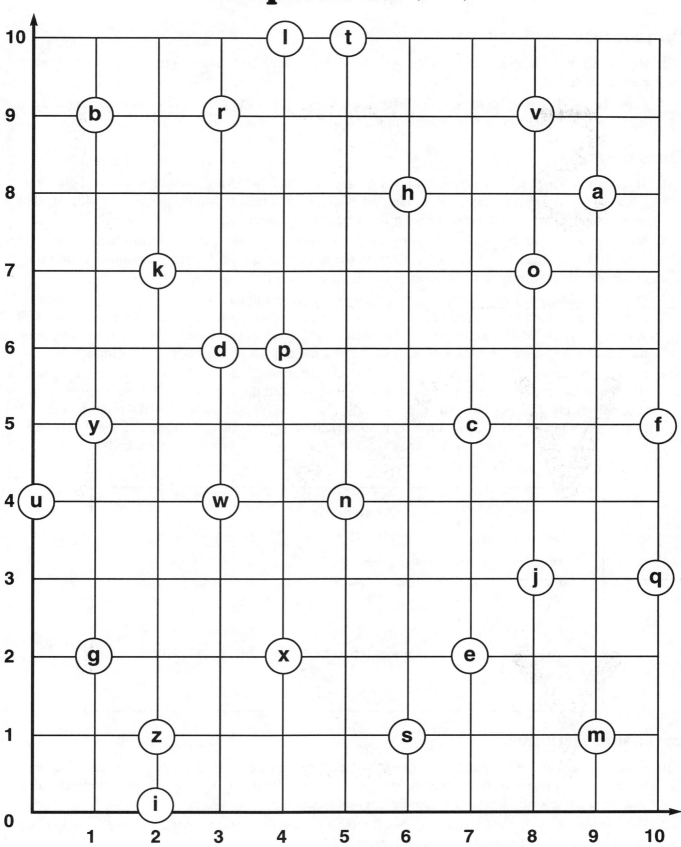

Number Words

Preparation:

1. Reproduce the number word cards (pages 105–106) and the coordinate graph (page 107) for each pair of students.

2. Glue the number word cards onto construction paper. Allow the glue to dry. Then laminate, cut out, and place each set in a reclosable plastic bag.

Directions:

1. Tell students that they are going to play a game to practice matching number words and numerals while using coordinate graphs. Explain that each pair of students will be given a set of cards that show number words and a coordinate graph that shows numerals.

2. Model how to play the game. Begin by shuffling the number word cards. Place the cards face down. Demonstrate how to pick a card from the top of the stack, identify the number word on it, and match that word with the correct numeral on the coordinate graph.

3. On the chalkboard, write the coordinates for the matching numeral. Be sure students understand that they must move to the right for the first number and then up for the second number. If students have difficulty remembering this, use a highlighter to color the numbers at the bottom of the coordinate graph. Tell them to always start by moving along the highlighted numbers.

4. Have each pair of students take turns drawing a number word card from the stack and identifying the matching numeral on the graph. Ask students to record the coordinates for each numeral on separate sheets of paper. Remind them to write the numerals and answers in the order that the number word cards are drawn rather than numerical order. Challenge students to see if they can get all of the answers correct. You may wish to create answer key cards for students to check themselves at the end of the game.

Answer Key

one, 1—(5,6)	eight, 8—(8,3)	fifteen, 15—(3,10)
two, 2—(3,9)	nine, 9—(2,8)	sixteen, 16—(7,8)
three, 3—(2,1)	ten, 10—(6,4)	seventeen, 17—(3,4)
four, 4—(9,2)	eleven, 11—(7,10)	eighteen, 18—(10,1)
five, 5—(9,9)	twelve, 12—(1,7)	nineteen, 19—(1,3)
six, 6—(4,7)	thirteen, 13—(4,2)	twenty, 20—(10,10)
seven, 7—(1,5)	fourteen, 14—(8,5)	

Extension Activities:

1. Rather than using the number word cards, you can call out numbers at random and have students write the coordinates of the numerals, or students can write the number words in numerical order and write the coordinates for the matching numerals.

2. Have students work with partners to develop their own games using coordinate graphs to practice matching additional number words and numerals.

Number Words (cont.)

one	two
three	four
five	six
seven	eight
nine	ten

Number Words *(cont.)*

eleven	twelve
thirteen	fourteen
fifteen	sixteen
seventeen	eighteen
nineteen	twenty

Number Words (cont.)

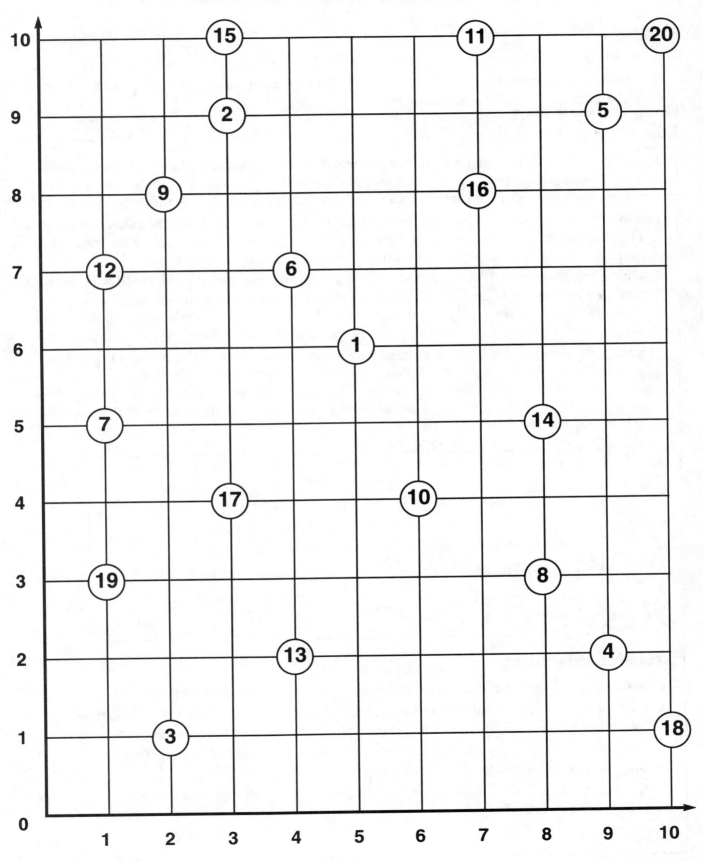

Shapes

Preparation:

1. Reproduce the shape cards (pages 109–110) and the coordinate graph (page 111) for students.
2. Glue the shape cards onto construction paper. Allow the glue to dry. Then laminate, cut out, and place each set in a reclosable plastic bag.

Directions:

1. Tell students that they are going to practice matching the names and pictures of shapes while using coordinate graphs. Explain that each student will be given a set of cards that show the names and pictures of the shapes and a coordinate graph that shows just the pictures of the shapes.
2. Model how to do the activity. Begin by shuffling the shape cards. Place the cards face down. Demonstrate how to pick a card from the top of the stack, identify the name of the shape shown on it, and match that shape with the correct one on the coordinate graph.
3. On the chalkboard, write the coordinates for the matching picture. Be sure students understand that they must move to the right for the first number and then up for the second number. If students have difficulty remembering this, use a highlighter to color the numbers at the bottom of the coordinate graph. Tell them to always start by moving along the highlighted numbers.
4. Each time students match the shape card with its picture on the graph, they should record the coordinates on their own papers. Remind them to write the names of the shapes and their answers in the order that the shape cards are drawn. Challenge students to see if they can get all of the answers correct. You may wish to create answer key cards for students to check themselves at the end of this activity.

Answer Key

Sphere—(1,1)	Square—(7,2)
Cube—(5,5)	Pentagon—(3,5)
Circle—(1,7)	Hexagon—(7,4)
Triangle—(6,7)	Octagon—(4,2)
Rectangle—(2,3)	Pyramid—(8,8)

Extension Activities:

1. Assign partners and ask students to do the coordinate graph activity described above.
2. Invite students to make additional shape cards and draw pictures of these shapes on their coordinate graphs. Tell them to add these shape names and coordinates to their answers.
3. Have students help you create a real graph, using plastic or wooden shapes. This activity can be used for two- and/or three-dimensional shapes.
4. Allow students to cut out shapes from construction paper. Tell them to use the shapes to create collages or mosaics. Display the students' artwork.

Shapes (cont.)

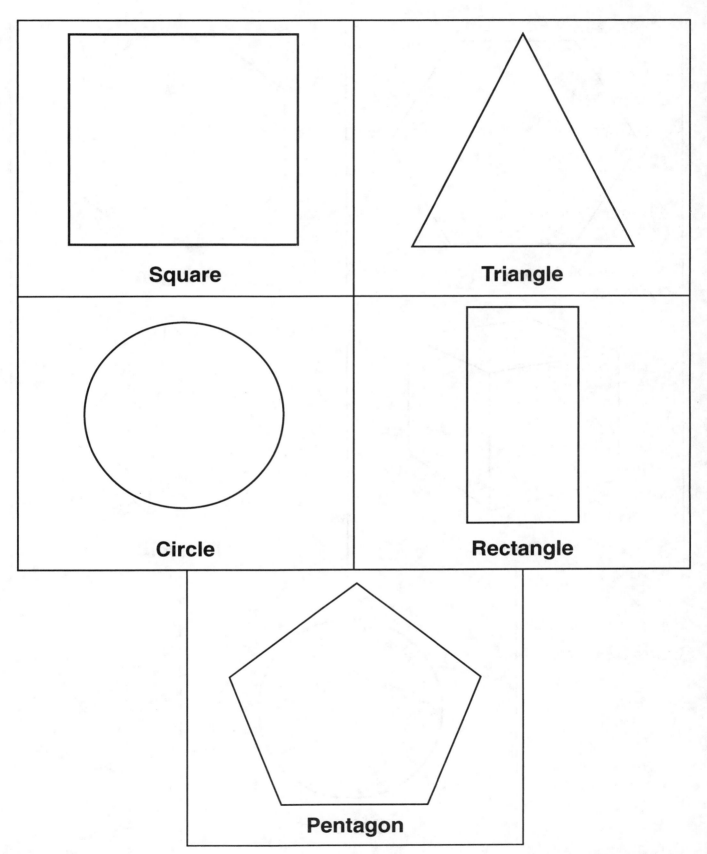

Square

Triangle

Circle

Rectangle

Pentagon

Shapes (cont.)

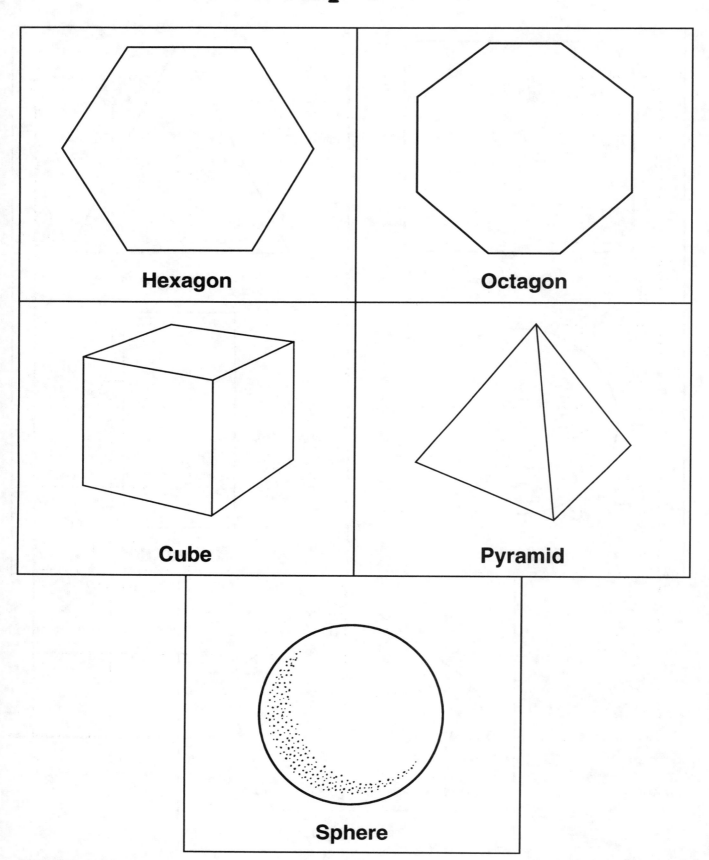

Hexagon

Octagon

Cube

Pyramid

Sphere

Shapes *(cont.)*

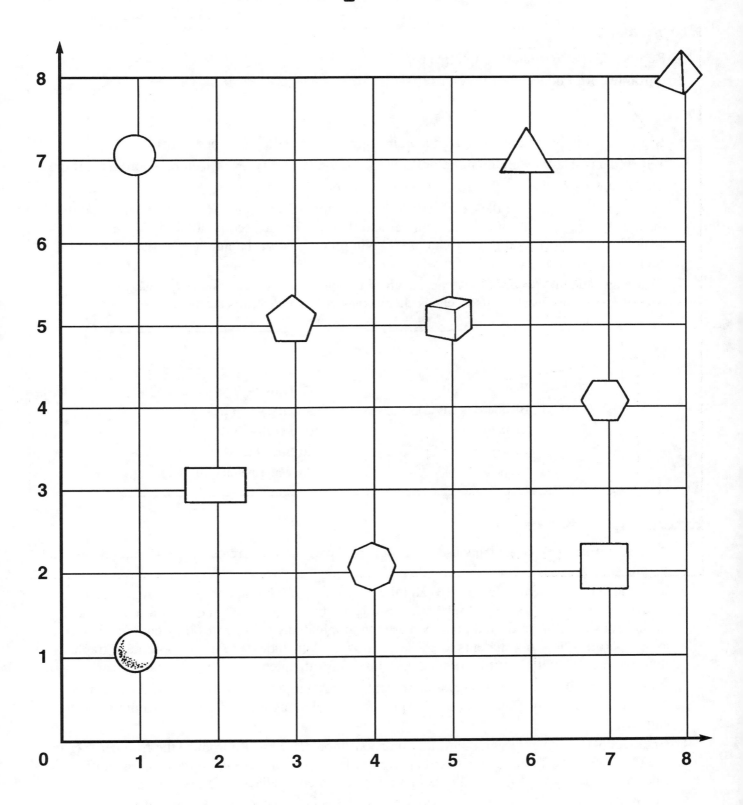

Fruit

Preparation:

1. Reproduce the coordinate graph (page 114) for students.
2. **Optional:** Reproduce the fruit cards (page 113) for students.

Directions:

1. Begin this activity by having students brainstorm a list of different types of fruit.
2. Tell students that they are going to practice locating different types of fruit on coordinate graphs.
3. Model how to do the activity, using the wall or floor coordinate graph.
4. On the chalkboard, write the coordinates for the picture of an apple. Remind students that they must move to the right for the first number and then up for the second number. If they have difficulty remembering this, they can use a highlighter to color the numbers at the bottom of the coordinate graph as a reminder for where to start.
5. Challenge students to see if they can get all of the answers correct. You may wish to create answer key cards for students to check themselves at the end of this activity.

Answer Key

1. Apple—(1,8)
2. Banana—(3,6)
3. Blueberries—(7,5)
4. Cantaloupe—(3,3)
5. Cherry—(4,5)
6. Grapes—(8,1)
7. Kiwi—(6,1)
8. Lemon—(3,0)
9. Orange—(2,2)
10. Peach—(1,4)
11. Strawberry—(5,3)
12. Watermelon—(6,7)

Extension Activities:

1. Assign partners. Have students use the fruit cards (page 113) to create their own coordinate wall graph.
2. Reproduce the fruit cards (page 113) and the coordinate graph (page 9) for students. Have students make a game similar to the one described on page 108. Ask them to cut out the pictures of the fruit from the cards and glue them on the graph at any coordinates they choose. Then assign partners or allow students to chose their own. Tell students to trade coordinate graphs with their partners. Invite them to write the coordinates for the pictures of fruit on each other's graphs.
3. Provide magazines and newspapers for students to cut out pictures of fruit. Invite students to make a class mural of fruit pictures. Display the mural along a wall in the classroom or in the cafeteria.
4. Obtain cookbooks that provide information about food calories. Reproduce the fruit cards (page 113) for students. Tell students to cut apart the cards. Ask them to identify the number of calories in each type of fruit and note that information on the backs of the cards.
5. Create the same kinds of activities as described above using vegetables instead of fruit.
6. Have students use coordinate grids to plan fruit, vegetable, or flower gardens.

Fruit (cont.)

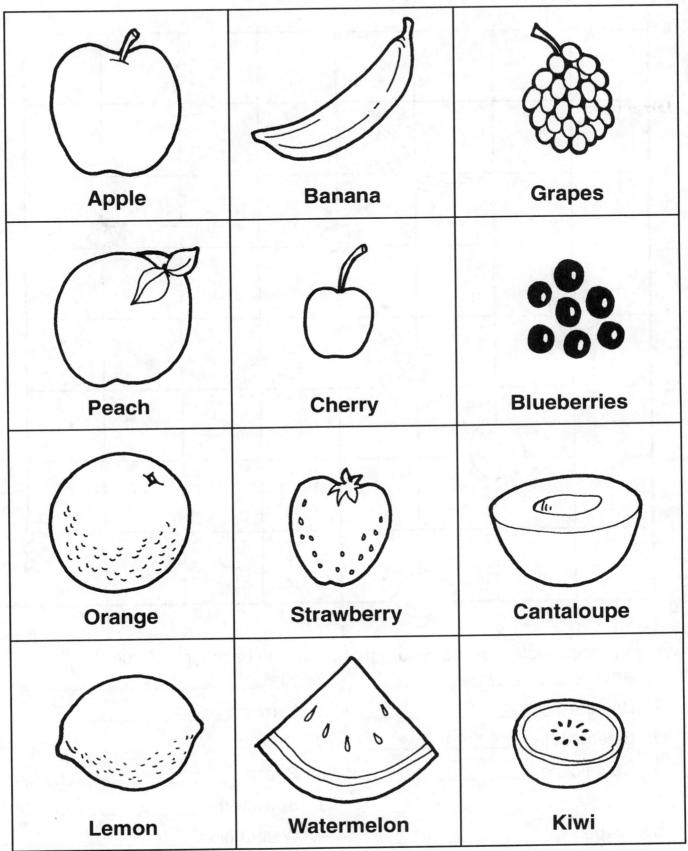

Apple	**Banana**	**Grapes**
Peach	**Cherry**	**Blueberries**
Orange	**Strawberry**	**Cantaloupe**
Lemon	**Watermelon**	**Kiwi**

113

#2007 Math Explorations

Fruit *(cont.)*

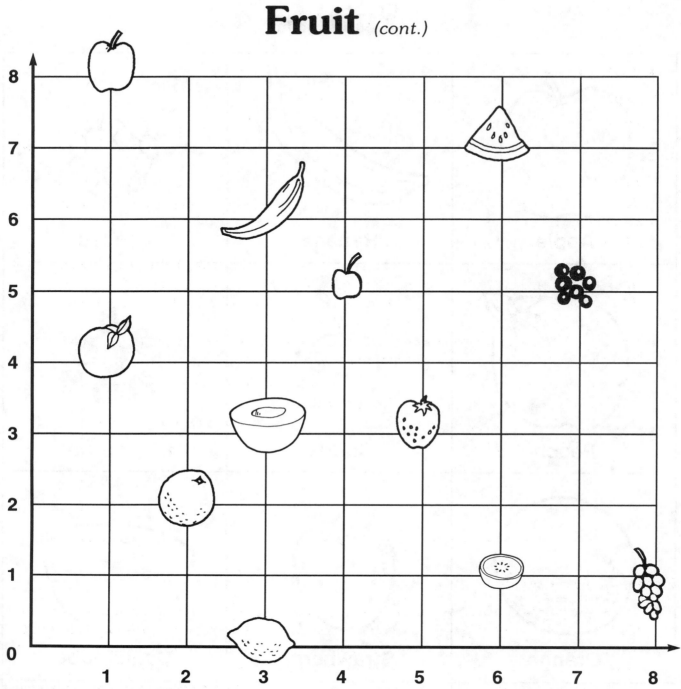

Write the coordinates for the picture that goes with each type of fruit.

1. Apple _____

2. Banana _____

3. Blueberries _____

4. Cantaloupe _____

5. Cherry _____

6. Grapes _____

7. Kiwi _____

8. Lemon _____

9. Orange _____

10. Peach _____

11. Strawberry _____

12. Watermelon _____

Sports

Preparation:

1. Reproduce the coordinate graph (page 117) for students.
2. **Optional:** Reproduce the sports cards (page 116) for students.

Directions:

1. Begin this activity by having students brainstorm a list of sports.
2. Tell students that they are going to practice locating different pictures related to sports on coordinate graphs.
3. Model how to do the activity, using the wall or floor coordinate graph.
4. On the chalkboard, write the coordinates for the picture of a baseball. Remind students that they must move to the right for the first number and then up for the second number. If they have difficulty remembering this, they can use a highlighter to color the numbers at the bottom of the coordinate graph as a reminder for where to start.
5. Challenge students to see if they can get all of the answers correct. You may wish to create answer key cards for students to check themselves at the end of this activity.

Answer Key

1. Baseball—(4,1)
2. Basketball—(3,4)
3. Bowling—(4,3)
4. Football—(1,2)
5. Golf—(3,2)
6. Gymnastics—(5,2)
7. Soccer—(1,4)
8. Swimming—(4,4)
9. Tennis—(2,1)
10. Track & Field—(2,3)

Extension Activities:

1. Reproduce the sport cards (page 116). Assign partners. Allow time for each pair of students to work on the wall or floor graph by themselves. Tell one student from each pair to use the sport cards to create the wall or floor coordinate graph. Have the other student from each pair determine the coordinates of the cards. Then encourage the partners to change roles.
2. Provide sports stickers (TCM 1241) for students to use. Write the names of the sports represented by the stickers. Have students vote on their favorite sports. Ask them to use the stickers to make pictographs that show how the class voted.
3. Have students name their favorite athletes. If possible, help students locate information about these sports figures in biographies, almanacs, or on the backs of collectors' sports cards. Allow time for students to share what they have learned about these athletes.
4. Divide the class into cooperative learning groups. Ask each group of students to choose a simple game that they can teach the class. Have students work together to write compositions that tell how to play the games they have chosen. Then allow time for each group to read the composition and teach the game to the class. You may wish to challenge students by asking them to create new games that they can teach the class to play.

Sports (cont.)

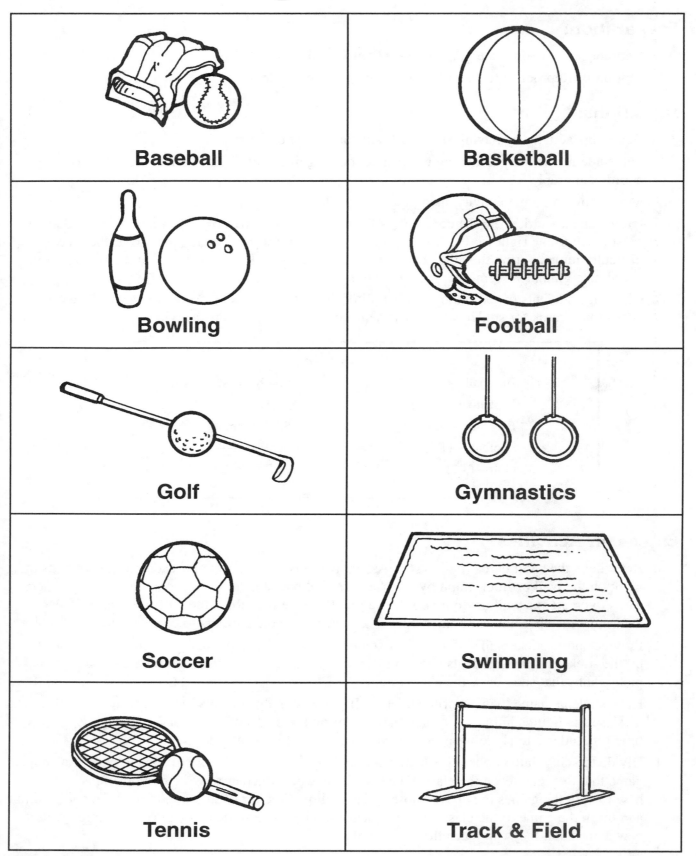

Baseball

Basketball

Bowling

Football

Golf

Gymnastics

Soccer

Swimming

Tennis

Track & Field

Sports *(cont.)*

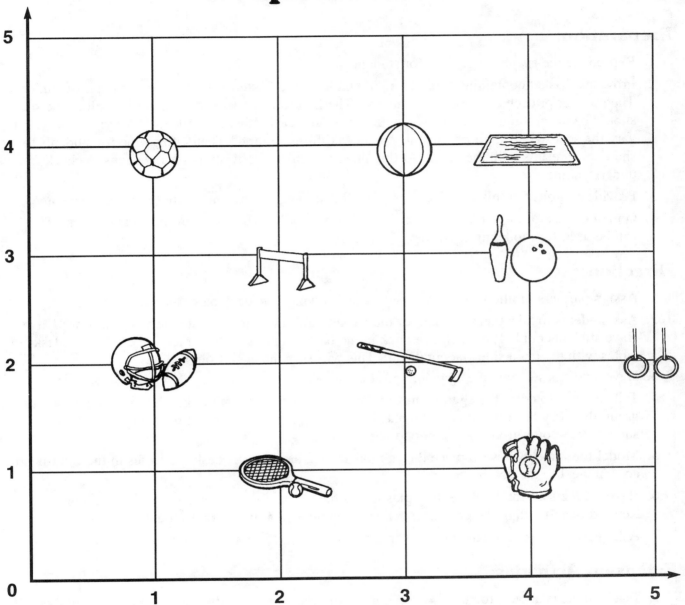

Write the coordinates for the picture that goes with each sport.

1. Baseball _____
2. Basketball _____
3. Bowling _____
4. Football _____
5. Golf _____

6. Gymnastics _____
7. Soccer _____
8. Swimming _____
9. Tennis _____
10. Track & Field _____

Easter Eggs

Preparation:

1. Reproduce the graph (page 120) for students.
2. Provide a basket containing four colors of small plastic Easter eggs in it for each pair of students. The number of each color of egg can vary. The first time students do this activity all of the sets should be exactly the same. This way they can help each other if needed. Later you may wish to vary the sets so each pair of students creates a different graph. Then allow time for students to share their results with the class. At this time, you may also wish to ask questions to check for understanding.
3. Provide crayons that match the colors of the Easter eggs if students do not already have some.
4. Obtain one set of large plastic Easter eggs that match the four colors of the smaller ones. These can be used for modeling each step of the activity.

Directions:

1. Assign partners or allow students to select their own. Give each pair a basket with eggs.
2. Ask students to take their eggs out of the basket. Tell them to separate each egg into two halves. Have students put half of each egg back in the basket and place the other halves on their desks or tables with the open sides facing down. This will stop the eggs from rolling.
3. Have students separate the eggs into groups by colors.
4. Tell students to color the egg pictures in the left-hand column on the graph to match each color group that they have made with the plastic Easter eggs. Point out that these pictures are used to show which color groups are going to appear on the graph.
5. Model for students how to place the egg halves that are on their desks or tables in the right-hand column next to the correct color.
6. Have students correctly place their plastic egg halves on the graph according to the colors. Remind them to align the eggs as much as possible so that their graphs are easy to read.
7. Ask questions to check students' understanding.

Extension Activities:

1. Teach students about probability using the plastic Easter eggs. After determining the number of each egg color have students make predictions about which colors are most likely, least likely, or have an equal chance to be drawn. *(The color with the greatest number will most likely be drawn. The one with the fewest will least likely be drawn. Colors that have the same number will have an equal chance of being drawn.)*
2. Reproduce the egg patterns (page 119). Have students color the patterns and use them to create wall or floor pictographs as well as individual pictographs to represent the number of Easter eggs in their baskets.
3. Help students decorate real or plastic eggs for Easter.

Easter Eggs (cont.)

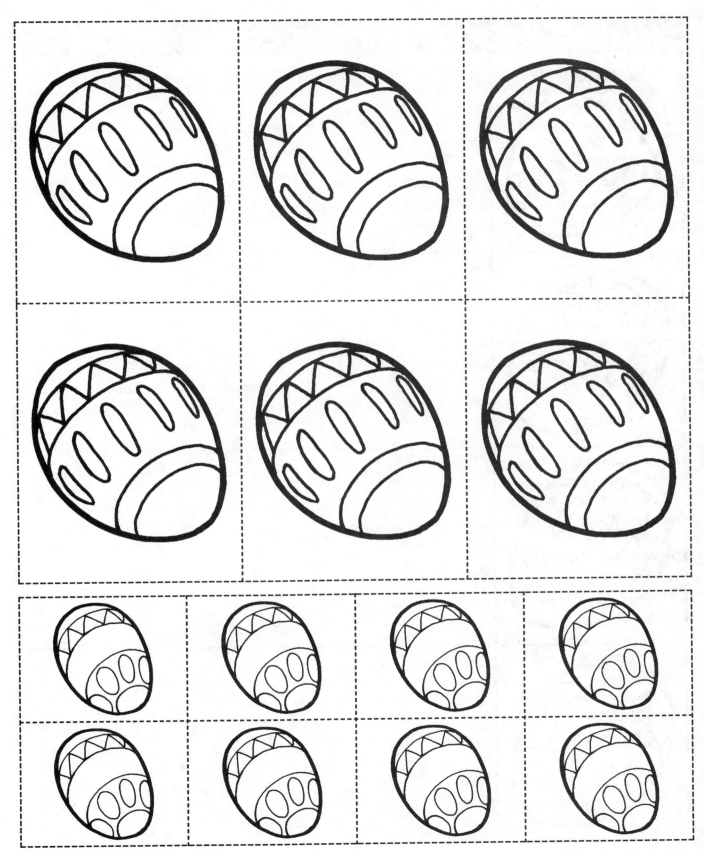

Easter Eggs (cont.)

EASTER EGG COLORS	

120

Bear Counters

Preparation:

1. Provide red, blue, green, and yellow bear counters for students. You may wish to make sets of these and place them in reclosable plastic bags.
2. Reproduce the graph (page 123) for students.
3. **Optional:** Cut out the bear patterns (page 122) and color them. Place them on a wall coordinate graph so students can check their own answers.

Directions:

1. Provide each student with a coordinate graph and some red, blue, green, and yellow bear counters. Allow students to sort the counters by color.
2. Have students place their bear counters on their coordinate graphs as you call out the colors and coordinates shown below. Circulate around the class to check their answers.

red (1, 2)	blue (1, 0)	green (2, 5)	blue (3, 1)	green (0, 0)
yellow (4, 4)	green (5, 3)	red (5, 2)	yellow (2, 3)	yellow (0, 4)

3. **Optional:** Use the wall coordinate graph and the bear counter patterns to show students the correct answers.

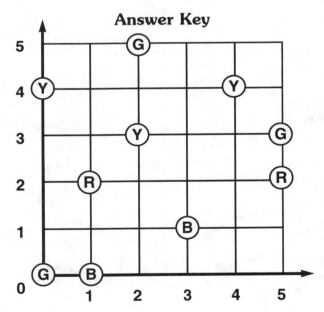

Answer Key

Extension Activities:

1. Read any version of *Goldilocks and the Three Bears.* Encourage students to use their bear counters to retell the story.
2. Allow students to take turns naming the colors and coordinates as the others place their bear counters on their coordinate graphs.
3. Have students sort their bear counters by color. Ask them to record the data on bar graphs (page 7 or 8).

Bear Counters *(cont.)*

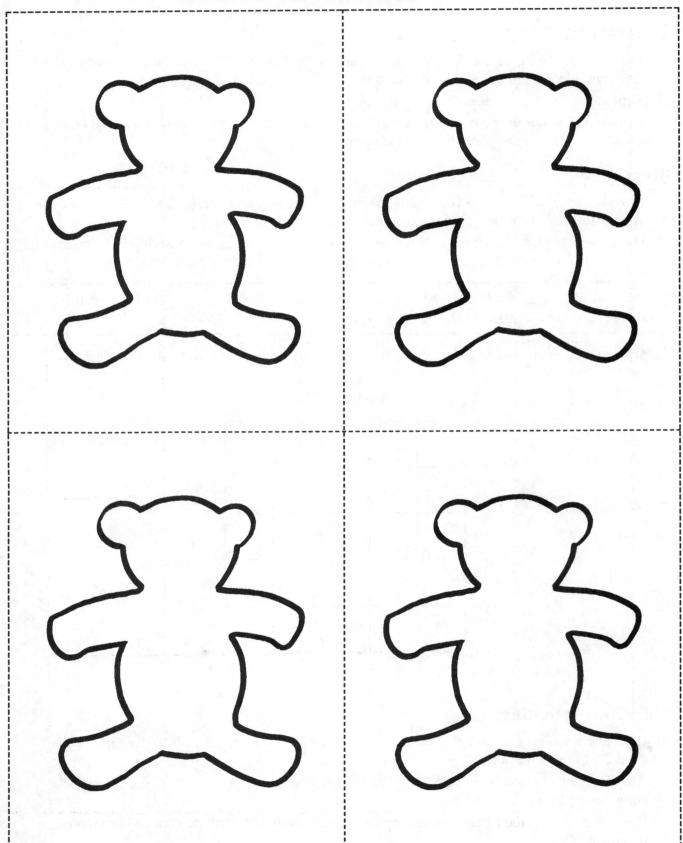

Bear Counters *(cont.)*

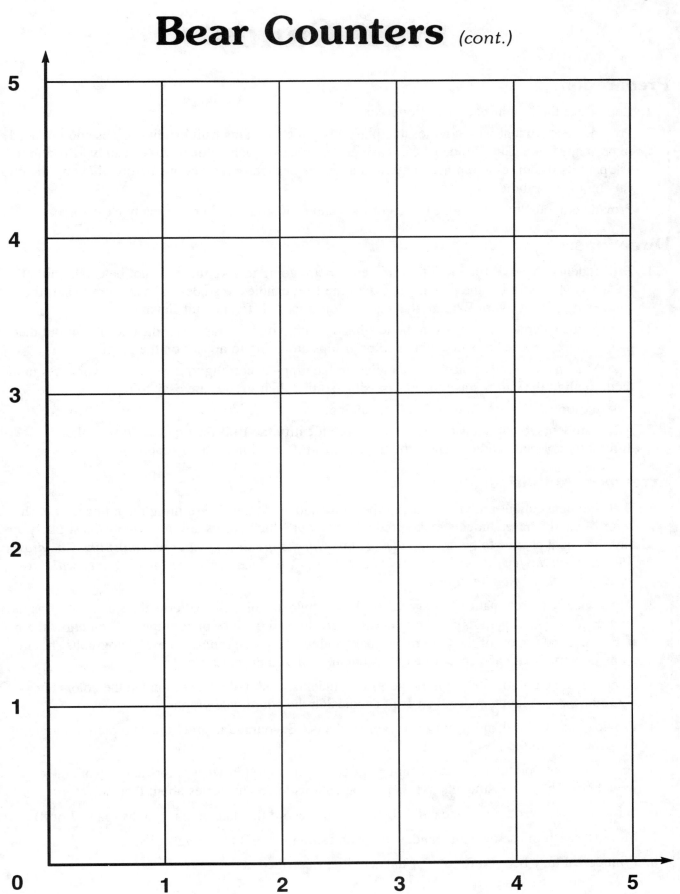

Fruit Candy

Preparation:

1. Reproduce the graph (page 126) for students.
2. Provide each student with a reclosable plastic bag that contains fruit candies. These do not need to be shaped like fruit. Students can have any number of each color/flavor of candy. Be sure to ask parents if their children have any food allergies or dietary restrictions before allowing them to eat any of the candies.
3. Provide crayons that match the colors of the candies if students do not already have some.

Directions:

1. Tell students ahead of time that the candies you are going to give them cannot be eaten until after the activity. Distribute the plastic bags with the fruit candies to students. Ask them to sort the candies by color/flavor. Explain that each color is for a different fruit flavor.
2. Have students color the circles in the left-hand column on the graph as indicated. Point out that these circles are used to show which color groups are going to appear on the graph.
3. Have students correctly place their candies on the graph according to the colors/flavors. Remind them to align the candies as much as possible so that their graphs are easy to read.
4. Ask questions to check students' understanding.
5. Allow students to eat the candies. Tell them to identify the fruit flavors that go with the differently colored candies. Have them write this information on their graphs.

Extension Activities:

1. Teach students about probability using the fruit candies. After determining the number of each color of candy, have students make predictions about which colors are most likely, least likely, or have an equal chance to be drawn. *(The color with the greatest number will most likely be drawn. The one with the fewest will least likely be drawn. Colors that have the same number will have an equal chance of being drawn.)*
2. Reproduce the circle patterns (page 125). Have students color the patterns the same colors as the fruit candies. Ask them to use the patterns to create wall or floor pictographs. Then allow them to use reduced copies of the patterns to make individual pictographs. These pictographs should show how many of each color of candy students had in their plastic bags.
3. Reproduce the coordinate graph (page 9) for students. Ask volunteers to name the colors and coordinates as students place their fruit candies on the coordinate graphs.
4. Provide poster board and fruit candies for students. Encourage them to create a picture by gluing the candies onto the poster board.
5. Ask students to pretend they are fruit candies. Ask them to tell what colors and flavors they would be. Then have students use their imaginations to create stories about themselves.
6. Have students sort their fruit candies by color and record the data on bar graphs (page 7 or 8).
7. You may wish to use the fruit candies to teach estimation and rounding skills.
8. Fruit cereal may be used for any of the activities described above.

Fruit Candy *(cont.)*

Red

Purple

Green

Yellow

Orange

Blue

Fruit Candy *(cont.)*

FRUIT CANDY COLORS AND FLAVORS	
Red ( ) **Flavor:**_____	
Purple ( ) **Flavor:**_____	
Green ( ) **Flavor:**_____	
Yellow ( ) **Flavor:**_____	
Orange ( ) **Flavor:**_____	
Blue ( ) **Flavor:**_____	

Candy-Coated Chocolates

Preparation:

1. Purchase candy-coated chocolates for students. (**Note:** M&M's® work well.) If you buy a large package, you can make individual packages by placing two or three of each color (red, blue, green, yellow, orange, and brown) in reclosable plastic bags. Be sure each bag contains the same amount of each color. Keep extra chocolates in a separate bag to replace any that students drop during the activity.

2. Be sure to ask parents if their children have any food allergies or dietary restrictions.

3. Reproduce the coordinate graph (page 129) for students.

4. **Optional:** Cut out large (red, blue, green, yellow, orange, brown) construction paper circles or color and cut the patterns (page 128) for use on a wall coordinate graph.

Directions:

1. Tell students ahead of time that the candies you are going to give them cannot be eaten until after the activity. Provide each student with a coordinate graph and an individual package of candy-coated chocolates. Allow students to take out the chocolates and sort them by color.

2. Have students place their candies on their coordinate graphs as you call out the colors and coordinates shown below. Circulate around the class to check each student's answers.

red (1, 5)	blue (3, 4)	green (4, 2)	brown (2, 1)	yellow (4, 5)
yellow (2, 3)	green (0, 3)	orange (1, 1)	red (3, 2)	brown (5, 0)

3. **Optional:** Use the wall coordinate graph and the patterns or construction paper circles to show students the correct answers.

Answer Key

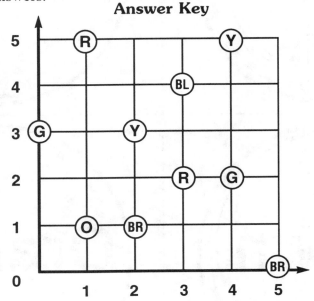

Extension Activities:

1. Allow students to take turns naming the colors and coordinates as the others place their chocolates on their coordinate graphs.

2. Have students sort their chocolates by color and record the data on bar graphs (page 7 or 8).

Candy-Coated Chocolates (cont.)

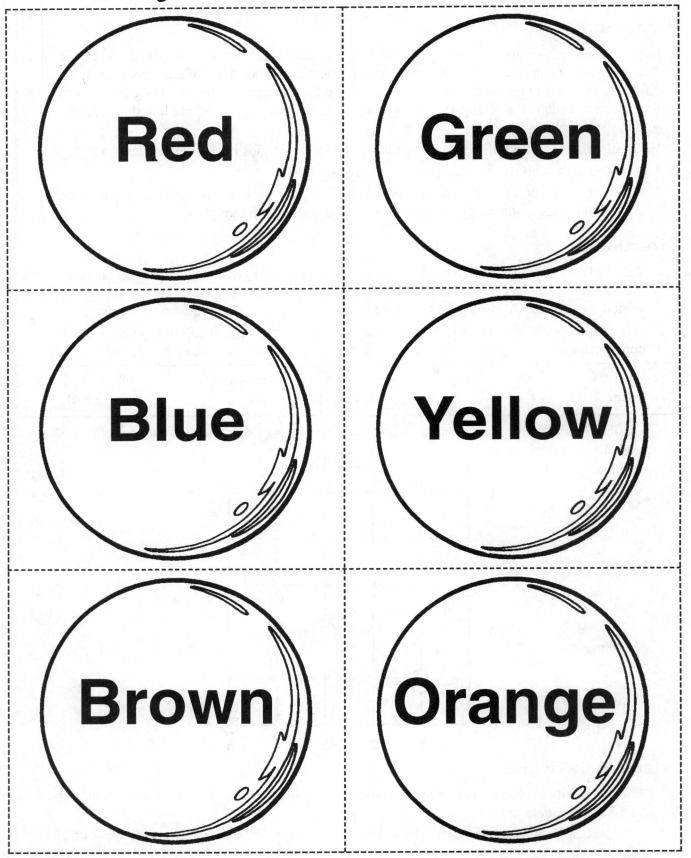

128

Candy-Coated Chocolates *(cont.)*

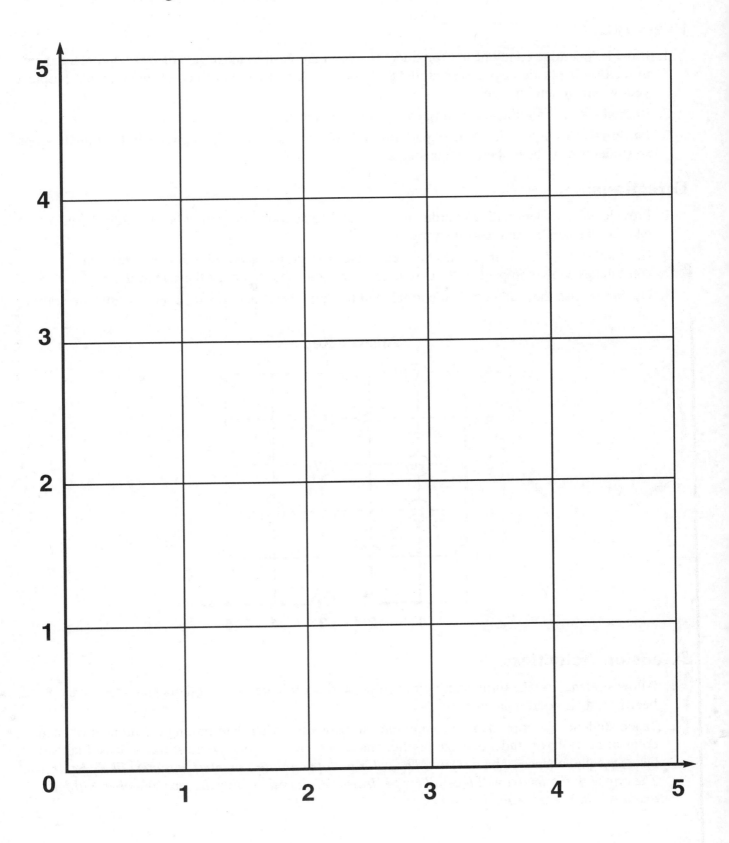

#2007 Math Explorations

Valentine Candy Hearts

Preparation:

1. Provide Valentine candy hearts for students. You may wish to make sets of these and place them in reclosable plastic bags. Each student will need at least two of each color: white, pink, purple, yellow, green, and orange.

2. Reproduce the coordinate graph (page 132) for students.

3. **Optional:** Cut out the large heart patterns and color them. Place them on a wall coordinate graph so students can check their own answers.

Directions:

1. Provide each student with a coordinate graph and some Valentine candy hearts. Allow students to take out the candies and sort them by color.

2. Have students place their candies on their coordinate graphs according to the colors and coordinates shown on page 132. Circulate around the class to check their answers.

3. **Optional:** Use the wall coordinate graph and the large heart patterns to show students the correct answers.

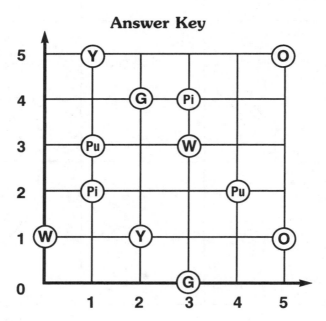

Answer Key

Extension Activities:

1. Allow students to take turns naming the colors and coordinates as the others place their candy hearts on their coordinate graphs.

2. Teach students about probability, using the candy hearts. After determining the number of each color of heart, have students make predictions about which colors are most likely, least likely, or have an equal chance to be drawn. *(The color with the greatest number will most likely be drawn. The one with the fewest will least likely be drawn. Colors that have the same number will have an equal chance of being drawn.)*

Valentine Candy Hearts *(cont.)*

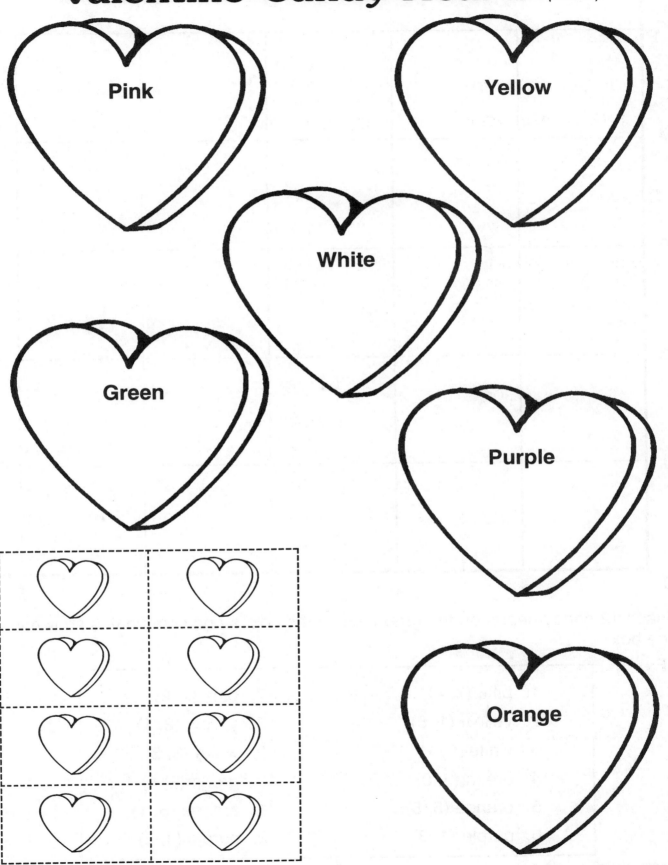

Valentine's Candy Hearts (cont.)

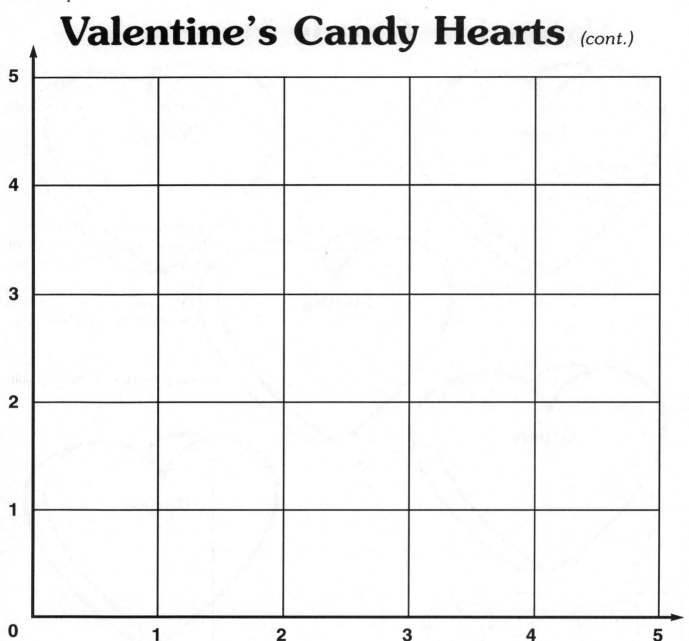

Place 12 candy hearts on the graph, using the colors and coordinates shown in the box.

1. pink (3, 4)	7. pink (1, 2)
2. yellow (1, 5)	8. yellow (2, 1)
3. white (0, 1)	9. white (3, 3)
4. green (3, 0)	10. green (2, 4)
5. orange (5, 5)	11. orange (5, 1)
6. purple (1, 3)	12. purple (4, 2)

132

Marshmallows

Preparation:

1. Purchase miniature colored marshmallows for students. If you buy a large package, you can make individual packages by placing some of each color in reclosable plastic bags. Be sure to ask parents if their children have any food allergies or dietary restrictions.

2. Reproduce the coordinate graph (page 135) for students.

Directions:

1. Tell students ahead of time that the marshmallows you are going to give them cannot be eaten until after the activity. Provide each student with a coordinate graph and an individual package of miniature colored marshmallows. Allow students to take out the marshmallows and sort them by color.

2. Explain that the specific coordinates are given at the bottom of page 135. Students may choose to make any color patterns they like. However, they must record the color of the marshmallow they use for each set of coordinates.

3. Point out that after students have placed their marshmallows on the graph, they will discover they have written a word (HI). Ask them to write the secret word on the line provided. Then they can eat their marshmallows.

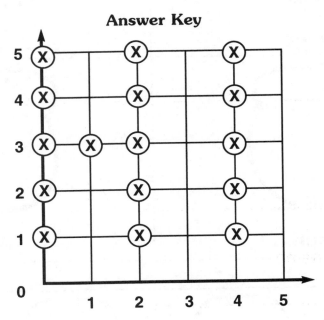

Answer Key

Extension Activities:

1. Allow students to take turns naming the colors and coordinates as the others place their marshmallows on their coordinate graphs.

2. Have students sort their marshmallows by color and record the data on bar graphs.

3. Use the miniature colored marshmallows to teach estimation and rounding.

Marshmallows *(cont.)*

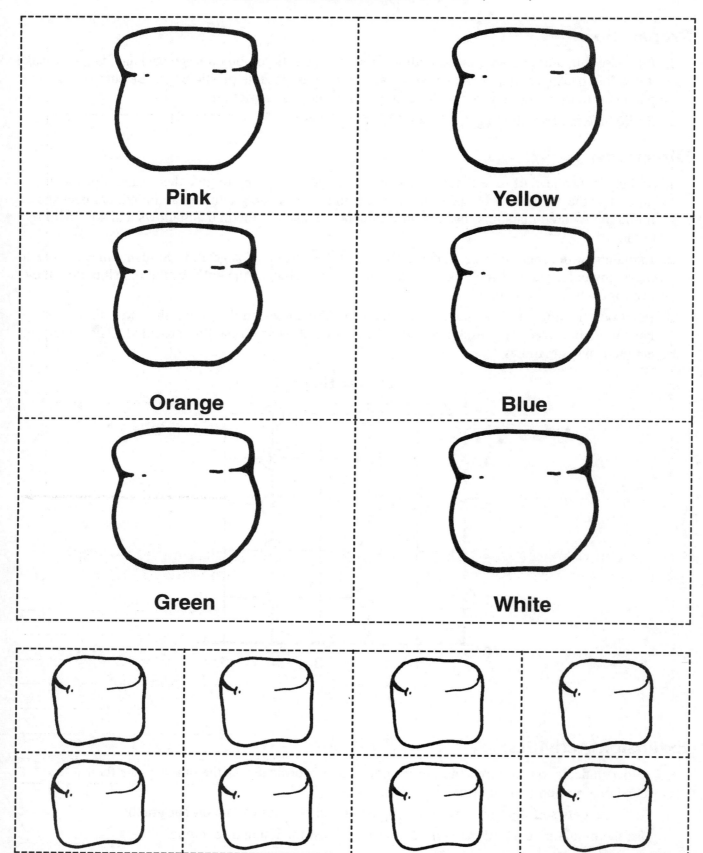

Pink

Yellow

Orange

Blue

Green

White

Marshmallows (cont.)

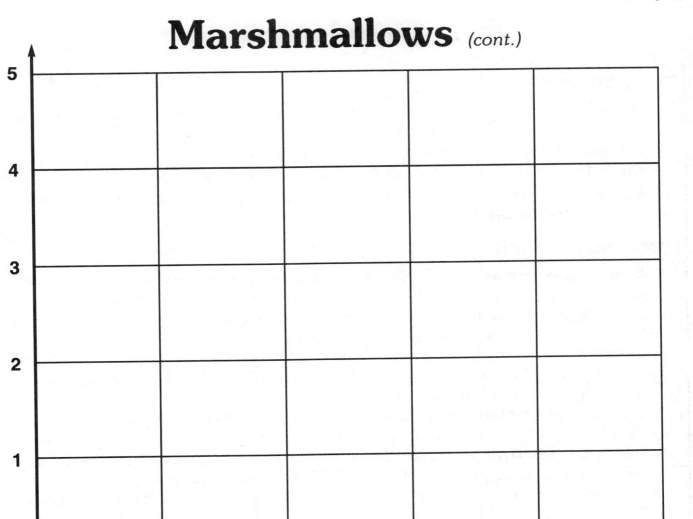

Use the coordinates shown below to place your marshmallows on the graph. For each set of coordinates, write the color of the marshmallow you use.

1. (0, 1) _____
2. (4, 4) _____
3. (2, 3) _____
4. (4, 2) _____
5. (1, 3) _____
6. (0, 5) _____
7. (4, 1) _____
8. (2, 5) _____

9. (2, 2) _____
10. (0, 4) _____
11. (2, 4) _____
12. (4, 5) _____
13. (0, 2) _____
14. (2, 1) _____
15. (0, 3) _____
16. (4, 3) _____

Now look at the secret word you have written with your marshmallows.
What is it? _____

       #2007 Math Explorations

Popcorn

Preparation:

1. Purchase colored unpopped popcorn for students. Make individual packages by placing some in reclosable plastic bags. Keep extra popcorn in a separate bag in case it is needed.
2. Reproduce the coordinate graph (page 138) for students.
3. Obtain a copy of the book *The Popcorn Shop* by Alice Low (Scholastic, 1994).
4. **Optional:** Make some popcorn for students to eat. Ask parents if their children have any food allergies or dietary restrictions.

Directions:

1. Begin this activity by reading aloud the book *The Popcorn Shop*. Discuss the story with students.
2. Tell students ahead of time that they should NOT eat the unpopped popcorn. You may wish to make some popcorn for students to enjoy while they are working on this activity.
3. Provide each student with a coordinate graph and an individual package of colored unpopped popcorn. Allow students to take out the kernels of popcorn and sort them by color.
4. Explain to students that they are going to make their own designs, using the popcorn and their coordinate graphs. Encourage them to be creative.
5. Lead students to conclude that they should plan their design first, make changes, and then record the colors and coordinates on separate pieces of paper.
6. Point out that before they remove their designs from the graph, they should check to be sure they have accurately recorded the information so other students can recreate their designs.
7. Encourage students to make, answer keys for their original designs. This will make it easier for them to check other students recreations. You may wish to show students examples of answer keys (pages 127 and 130).
8. Allow time for students to trade papers and make each other's designs. Have the original designers check the accuracy of the recreations.

Extension Activities:

1. Allow students to take turns naming the colors and coordinates as the others place their popcorn kernels on their coordinate graphs.
2. Have students sort their popcorn kernels by color. Ask them to record the data on bar graphs (page 7 or 8).
3. Use the colored unpopped popcorn to teach estimation and rounding.
4. Ask students to pretend that they are popcorn kernels. Invite them to tell stories about their adventures as a piece of popcorn.
5. Encourage students to do research to learn about the history of popcorn.
6. Provide poster board and plenty of colored unpopped popcorn. Ask students to create pictures by gluing the kernels onto the poster board.

Popcorn *(cont.)*

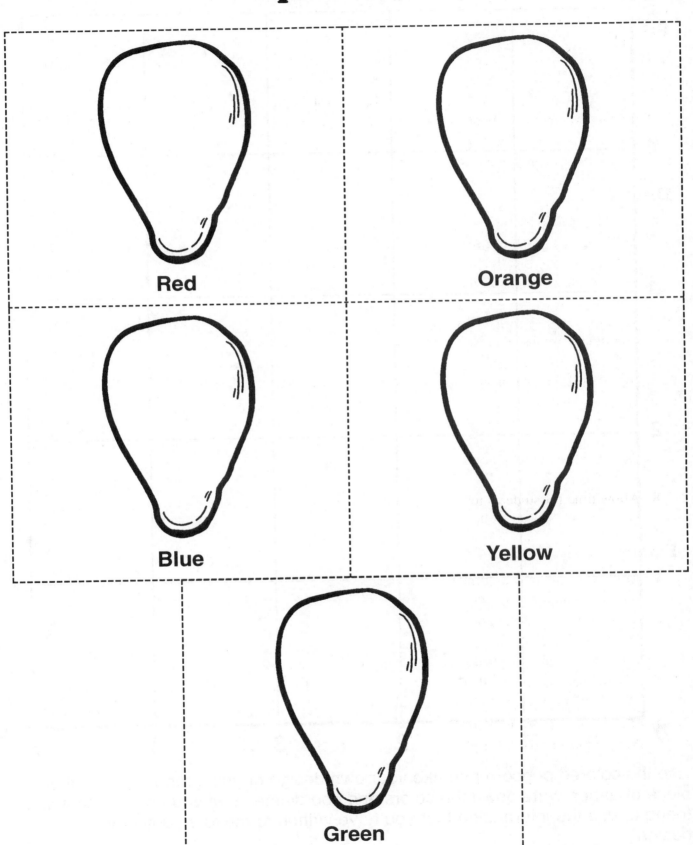

Red

Orange

Blue

Yellow

Green

Popcorn *(cont.)*

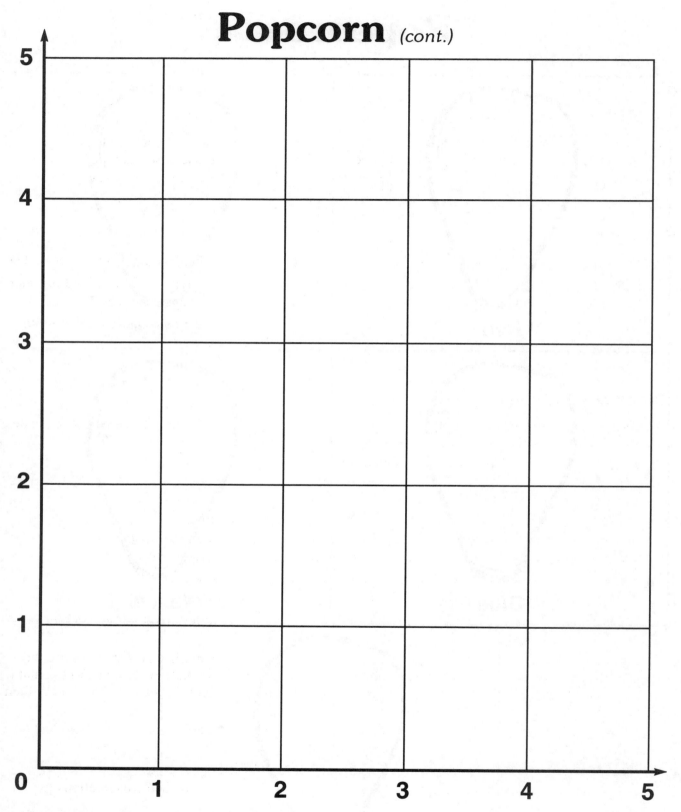

Use the colored popcorn to make your own design on this graph. On another piece of paper, write down the colors and coordinates that you use. Then ask a friend to use the information that you have written to make a copy of your design.

Holiday Bows

Preparation:

1. Reproduce the graph (page 141) for students.
2. Provide each student with a large reclosable plastic bag that contains small red, blue, and green bows. Students can have any number of each color of bow. Try to use bows that are approximately the same size, and be sure they are small enough to fit on the graph (page 141).
3. Provide crayons that match the colors of the bows if students do not already have some.

Directions:

1. Distribute the plastic bags with the holiday bows to students. Ask them to sort the bows by color.
2. Have students color the bows shown in the left-hand column on the graph as indicated. Point out that these pictures are used to show which color groups are going to appear on the graph.
3. Have students correctly place their bows on the graph according to the colors. Remind them to align the bows as much as possible so that their graphs are easy to read.
4. Ask questions to check students' understanding.

Extension Activities:

1. Use the bows to teach some simple algebraic concepts. Use the problems shown below or create some of your own.
   - Two red bows equal four. How much is each red bow worth? *(2)*
   - One red bow equals six. One red bow minus one green bow equals two. How much is the green bow worth? *(4)*
   - Two times one gold bow equals 14. How much is one gold bow worth? *(7)*
   - Five times one white bow equals zero. How much is one white bow worth? *(0)*
   - One blue bow equals three. How much are three blue bows worth? *(9)*
   - One half of a green bow is two. How much is one green bow worth? *(4)*
   - Two silver bows equal ten. How much are three silver bows worth? *(15)*
   - One red bow equals one. One red bow plus one green bow equals nine. How much is the green bow worth? *(8)*
2. Reproduce the bow patterns (page 140). Have students color the patterns. Ask them to use the patterns to create wall or floor pictographs. Then allow them to use patterns to make individual pictographs. These pictographs should show how many of each color of bow students had in their plastic bags.
3. Reproduce the coordinate graph (page 9) for students. Ask volunteers to name the colors and coordinates as students place their bows on their coordinate graphs.
4. Invite students to make decorations or pictures, using holiday bows.
5. Ask students to pretend they are holiday bows. Encourage them to use their imaginations to create stories about their holiday adventures as bows.
6. Have students sort their holiday bows by color. Ask them to record the data on bar graphs (page 7 or 8).

Holiday Bows *(cont.)*

Red

Green

White

Blue

Gold

Silver

Holiday Bows *(cont.)*

COLORS OF HOLIDAY BOWS	
Red	
Blue	
Green	

Pasta

Preparation:

1. Reproduce the two graphs (pages 143–144) for students.

2. Purchase three colors of three different types of pasta. You can make your own colored pasta by placing regular uncooked pasta, 15 drops of food coloring, and 2 tablespoons (30 mL) rubbing alcohol in a container with a lid. Shake the container. Remove the colored pasta and allow it to dry. The amount of food coloring affects the brightness of the color. Place the dried colored pasta in reclosable plastic bags. Make two sets of pasta for each student, one for each graphing activity. In each set, the number of each color and type of pasta can vary.

3. Provide glue if students do not already have some.

4. **Optional:** Reproduce the table (page 6), making two copies for each student.

Directions:

1. Begin by giving each student the graph on page 143, glue, and three pieces of pasta—one of each color. Tell students to glue one color of pasta in each box of the left-hand column. Point out that these pieces of pasta show which color groups are going to appear on the graph.

2. Distribute one bag of colored pasta to each student. Have students sort their pasta into groups by color. If you want students to record the data, distribute copies of the table.

3. Ask students to place their colored pasta in the appropriate rows on their graphs. Remind them to align the pasta as much as possible. Check for accuracy.

4. Tell students to carefully glue their pasta in place on their graphs. Allow the glue to dry.

5. Ask questions to check students' understanding.

6. Begin the next activity by giving each student the graph on page 144, glue, and three pieces of pasta—one of each type. Tell students to glue one type of pasta in each box of the left-hand column. Point out that these pieces of pasta show which types are going to appear on the graph.

7. Now distribute the bags with three types of pasta to students. Have them sort the pasta into groups by type, not color. If you want students to record the data, distribute copies of the table.

8. Ask students to place their types of pasta in the appropriate rows on their graphs. Remind them to align the pasta as much as possible. Check for accuracy.

9. Tell students to carefully glue their pasta in place on their graphs. Allow the glue to dry.

10. Ask questions to check students' understanding.

11. Display the graphs or encourage students to take them home to show family members.

Extension Activities:

1. Assign partners. Have students create pasta patterns for their partners to predict what will come next. Tell one student from each pair to arrange the pasta in patterns using the different colors and/or types. Have the other students guess what will come next if the patterns, continue.

2. Allow students to take turns naming the colors and coordinates as the others place their pasta on coordinate graphs.

Pasta *(cont.)*

COLORS OF PASTA	

Pasta *(cont.)*

TYPES OF PASTA